Prader-Willi Syndrome

Prader-Willi Syndrome

A Practical Guide

Jackie Waters

David Fulton Publishers
London

David Fulton Publishers Ltd
Ormond House, 26–27 Boswell Street, London WC1N 3JD

First published in Great Britain by David Fulton Publishers 1999

Note: The right of Jackie Waters to be identified as the author of this work has been asserted by her in accordance with the Copyright, Designs and Patents Act 1988

Copyright © Jackie Waters 1999

British Library Cataloguing in Publication Data
A catalogue record for this book is available from the British Library

ISBN 1–85346–614–X

Typeset by Textype Typesetters, Cambridge
Printed in Great Britain by Bell and Bain Ltd, Glasgow.

Contents

Preface

Prader-Willi Syndrome (PWS) is estimated to affect around one in 15,000 people. As it is relatively rare, it is unlikely that any one teacher will work with more than one or two pupils with the syndrome. There are no schools or colleges in the UK which specialise in PWS, although there are a few, mostly residential, which are building up a reputation in this field.

This book has been based on the work of researchers within the field of Prader-Willi syndrome, as well as considerable anecdotal information obtained from parents and carers from questionnaires and personal interviews. In order to obtain a bigger picture of children with PWS in a school situation, questionnaires were circulated to members of the Prader-Willi Syndrome Association (UK) to give to their child's teacher to complete. 101 questionnaires were completed and returned from teachers working with pupils with a wide ability and age range. I would like to thank those teachers who took the time to respond, as their replies have provided many valuable insights into educating children with PWS. However, bias may have occurred because only those parents who have a good home-school relationship are likely to have given the questionnaire to the teachers.

Children and young adults with PWS are likely to share some common characteristics, but the range of abilities is extremely wide, ranging from pupils who will pass GCSE (usually around grades D, E and F) to those who have severe learning difficulties. Nevertheless many aspects of teaching and classroom management cut across ability levels because of the dietary and behavioural aspects of the syndrome.

Using this book

Whilst I have tried to present different aspects of the syndrome within the most relevant age groups, there are bound to be instances where chronological age does not match that of the child's intellectual or emotional age. Thus, those working with individuals with PWS who have considerable intellectual delay may find it useful to read the chapters which pertain to children of a younger age when looking for ways to improve their performance.

Readers should also note that certain behavioural characteristics are more prevalent at certain ages, and they have been addressed within the relevant chapter(s). However, they may also manifest at other ages, and use of the index to find references to specific characteristics is therefore recommended.

Your help is needed

Because so little is collectively known about teaching children with PWS, this book represents just the beginning of the road towards better teaching methods and good practice. The PWSA (UK) would welcome feedback from anyone reading this book who can contribute ideas which have worked for their pupil with PWS, so that these can be shared with others in the future.

Note: All names of children have been changed to protect identities, except when quoting from references.

Jackie Waters
PWSA (UK)
May 1999

Acknowledgements

I am very grateful to all the teachers who took the time to complete questionnaires about their pupils. Special thanks to Toby Salt, Elizabeth Mussen, Deborah Thackray, Tara Chevalier and Carolynn Smith for providing child and student studies, and to those parents and youngsters with PWS who have given permission for their photographs and work to be used.

I would also like to thank Anne Richardson for her help in devising the questionnaire to teachers, and Rosemary Booth for her constructive comments about both the questionnaire and the content of this book. Thanks also to the PWSA (UK) and its members for their support.

Chapter 1

An Introduction to Prader-Willi Syndrome

This introduction provides an overview of the genetic, physical and psychological basis of Prader-Willi Syndrome (PWS). A general knowledge of these characteristics is essential, as the child with PWS needs to be understood within the context of the challenges placed on them by the syndrome. However, although many of the child's behavioural problems and cognitive abilities are explicable within this framework, other influences such as social and family environment, as well as hereditary factors, have their part to play in producing an overall picture of the child. These also need to be taken into account. Hence, while each child with PWS has some of the characteristics of the syndrome, they still remain very much individuals.

History, incidence and prevalence

Prader-Willi Syndrome (PWS) was first described by Swiss doctors, A. Prader, A. Labhart and H. Willi in 1956 (Prader *et al.* 1956). During the early 1960s, Dr Bernard Laurance reported several children in England with the features of what we now know to be Prader-Willi Syndrome, but it was not until later in that decade that doctors in the rest of the world became aware of it (Laurance 1961).

Even then, knowledge about the syndrome was scarce, tending to concentrate on those who were most severely affected, with the result that it was considered to be a syndrome which produced moderate to severe learning difficulties. Research has been more widely undertaken only within the last ten to fifteen years. The greatest advances have been made in the field of genetics, and it is much more recently that attention has begun to focus on the psychological and cognitive aspects of the syndrome. Since then, many cases have been reported of people whose intellectual abilities are within the borderline to low average range.

It is now acknowledged that Prader-Willi Syndrome has existed for centuries. A painting entitled 'La Monstrua' in the Museo del Prado in Spain is almost certainly that of little girl with PWS, and Langdown Down, who gave his name to Down's Syndrome, also wrote a report of a woman with features which fit the PWS characteristics (Ward 1997).

PWS occurs in all races and in both sexes. It is rarely hereditary, can occur in any family, but rarely occurs more than once in a family. Several cases of non-identical twins have been reported, where one twin has PWS and the other does not; more rare are identical twins with PWS. As far as is known, PWS is purely accidental, and no blame can be attached to either parents or doctors.

The true incidence is not known, but is estimated to be 1:15,000, based on calculations made in the USA and Norway. Previously, life expectancy was believed to be short, as it was thought that massive obesity in the early years of life could not be avoided. Now, with better management, people are living well into middle age. The oldest recorded person in the UK was aged 71 when she died (Carpenter 1994). However, without considerable effort on the part of all who live and work with individuals with PWS, death at a very early age still remains a threat.

The genetic background

The genetics of PWS are quite complicated. It can be caused by more than one type of genetic abnormality, but all result in an important piece of genetic coding being missed from the paternal chromosome 15.

The most common genetic abnormality, which is present in about 70 per cent of people with PWS, is called a deletion. This means that a minute piece of chromosome 15 inherited from the father is missing, probably damaged around the time of conception. It is thought that the missing piece contained several genes, some of which have now been identified. However, experts are still uncertain which genes, or rather the lack of information contained in them, are instrumental in causing PWS.

Another form of genetic anomaly is known as maternal disomy, and is present in around 25-30 per cent of people with PWS. It occurs when two chromosome 15s are inherited from the mother, and none from the father. Again, important genetic coding material is missing because of the absence of the paternal genes. Interestingly, where the situation is reversed, and the chromosome deletion is on the maternal chromosome, or two paternal chromosomes are present, an entirely different syndrome results. This is Angelman Syndrome, which causes severe learning difficulties and a range of severe physical disabilities. It manifests very differently to Prader-Willi Syndrome.

In a few other rare cases, translocations and other rare anomalies occur, which are the only hereditary cases of PWS.

There appear to be few differences between those who have deletion and disomy. However, researchers have found that those with deletion are more likely to have the typical PWS facial features and lighter hair and skin colouring than those with disomy. Skin picking, articulation abnormalities and a high pain threshold are also more likely in those with deletion (Cassidy *et al.* 1995), and research is still going on to identify other differences.

It is widely thought that most of the genetic information which is missing in PWS affects the hypothalamus, which controls and regulates many of the body's hormone mechanisms.

Diagnosis

The diagnosis of PWS has improved in recent years, partly because of increased awareness on the part of doctors, but also because chromosome tests are now done at a molecular level, and are therefore more able to detect the very small genetic anomalies which are present in PWS. Diagnosis is also carried out at the clinical level, which takes into account the various physical and mental characteristics of the child. There is still a very small minority of people who have most of the PWS characteristics but for whom no genetic anomaly can be found. These are often referred to as having 'atypical PWS'. There are also people who have some form of brain damage, either through disease or injury, which results in PWS-like characteristics. The management techniques which are appropriate for people with 'true' PWS are also appropriate for these groups.

An early diagnosis is very important, so that behaviour and dietary management can become part of the child's everyday life. However, some children do not receive a diagnosis until they are quite old – sometimes not until they are adults – and this can be very difficult for them and their parents to come to terms with. There are undoubtedly children who remain undiagnosed. If there is a suspicion the child has PWS, then they should be referred to a geneticist. Diagnostic criteria have been published (Holm *et al*. 1993) and are also available from the PWSA (UK).

Hypotonia (low muscle tone)

Major physical characteristics

Hypotonia is evident from birth, when babies usually present as very 'floppy'. As they have poor sucking ability, they can be very difficult to feed, and often need tube-feeding. This has implications in later life for possible speech problems. Low muscle tone continues throughout life, but can be helped with appropriate exercise, which also has a positive impact on weight control. Researchers are beginning to find that growth hormone treatment has a very beneficial effect on muscle tone in PWS (Eiholzer *et al*. 1998).

The low muscle tone varies in degree between individuals, but some may find holding a pencil difficult and most will have difficulty running, jumping and generally keeping up with their peers. Some children will be walking by the time they are two years old, others may still be having difficulty at the age of five or older.

Hypogonadism (immature sexual development)

Hypogonadism is more obvious from an early age in males than females. However, both sexes are likely to experience delayed or arrested puberty, and this has implications for sex education as well as peer relations.

Obesity

The tendency towards obesity, which can be life-threatening even in young children, is caused by an excessive appetite (hyperphagia, see below), coupled with a decreased calorific requirement owing to low energy expenditure levels. Obesity used to be considered an essential criterion for diagnosis of PWS, so prevalent was it amongst the PWS population; but with better parental management and medical guidance, more and more children with PWS are growing up who are not obese. This does not mean they will not become obese if controls are relaxed. It is a very careful balancing act to provide the individual with the necessary skills to maintain their weight at a reasonable level, and many are unable to do this at all without considerable outside intervention.

Typical facial characteristics

Many people with PWS, particularly those with a deletion, share certain facial characteristics, to the extent that a group of people together can look like brothers and sisters. These features include: a narrow forehead, 'almond-shaped' eyes with upward-slanting lower eyelids, and a down-turned mouth. Hair and skin colouring is often lighter than that of other members of the family.

Characteristics arising from hypothalamic dysfunction

The hormone-regulating properties of the hypothalamus affect growth, sexual development, appetite, and emotional control, all of which are affected in PWS.

Hyperphagia

Hyperphagia, or excessive appetite, is perhaps the most well-known feature of PWS. In contrast to the so-called 'first-stage' of the syndrome, where babies show little interest in feeding, sometime between the ages of two and five the interest in food begins to increase. However, it can vary considerably between individuals. While all will show a marked interest in food, a minority are relatively well able to control their food intake, whilst others will take every opportunity to access food. This may involve unacceptable behaviours such as rooting through waste-bins, stealing food from others' plates or out of their pockets, eating frozen food or pet food, or stealing money to buy food. Many are able to control their eating in supervised situations, but are unable to do so in unsupervised situations.

This behaviour can be understood in the context of the fact that it appears that the mechanism which informs most people when they have had enough to eat is faulty in people with PWS, and they feel hungry for most of the time, thus constantly thinking about, or seeking out, food (Holland 1998). Researchers are still unsure whether the variation in eating behaviour is due to differences in damage to the hypothalamus, other hereditary factors, or general education and management – both of carers and people with PWS.

Short stature

Many children with PWS are considerably shorter than their peers, and often have small hands and feet. However, increasingly, children are being prescribed growth hormone treatment which can often help with growth, as well as muscle tone. Some parents have also reported increased alertness and improved behaviour while their children have been on growth hormone. The average height for an adult who has not had growth hormone treatment is around 4'10" (145 cm) for women, and 5'2" (155 cm) for men. There are a few peopel with PWS who are taller than this, especially if they come from tall families.

Somnolence, tiredness

Sleeping patterns are also regulated by the hypothalamus, and these are often affected in people with PWS. As babies, they sleep for far longer than other babies, and can be difficult to rouse, even to feed. Young children require more naps, and even adults are prone to daytime sleepiness. This can be exacerbated by obesity. Sleep apnoea (cessation of breathing for short periods whilst asleep) can also interrupt sleeping patterns and, whilst this is more common in those who are obese, it has been noted in some children who are not. Researchers have also found evidence of unusual sleep patterns in individuals with PWS (Vela-Bueno *et al.* 1984).

Emotional instability

Individuals with PWS appear to have delayed or arrested emotional development, many exhibiting behaviours such as acting out, temper, tantrums, and stubbornness outbursts or which are normally evident in children of pre-school age but remain with the person with PWS all their life. Again, the degree to which this manifests varies considerably between one individual and another.

People with PWS do not always have the same medical reactions as most people. It is important that medical staff and first aiders are aware of these.

Other medical abnormalities sometimes associated with PWS

Adverse reaction to drugs

Although more is becoming known about the effects of drugs which react on the central nervous system of people with PWS (e.g. tranquillizers), there are still concerns that there may be adverse effects. Drugs to treat severely challenging behaviour in children are more widely used in the USA than in the UK, but need careful monitoring. Often, lower dosages than normal are required.

Prolonged drowsiness after routine anaesthesia, or complications arising from anaesthesia

If a child requires a general anaesthetic for any reason, the hospital should be informed that the child has PWS, and it can then take appropriate steps to monitor anaesthetic treatment. It is not unusual for a child to be drowsy for up to 24 hours after receiving anaesthetics. Very rarely, other complications may occur.

Irregular body thermostat

The hypothalamus also controls the body's internal temperature. This appears to be impaired in some people with PWS. Erratic behaviour and lethargy may become more pronounced in very hot or very cold weather, and it is important that the classroom temperature is neither too hot nor too cold. Normal childhood infections may induce a higher than normal temperature, sometimes resulting in fitting, but sometimes the temperature does not rise in response to sickness.

High pain threshold

Children with PWS may have an abnormal response to pain, which varies considerably between individuals. It is best to check with the parent or carer how each child reacts. Some will feel little or no pain, even with broken bones or stomach infections. Others may over-react to a small cut or graze, whilst ignoring the pain of a more serious illness. Some may complain of pain as an attention-seeking device. However, in the first place it is best to treat any complaint of pain seriously, as the child may have a serious illness or wound which needs treatment. One example is the child who was always 'crying wolf' about her illnesses, and was only listened to when she developed a lump in her stomach. It transpired that she had a blockage in her bowel (Waters 1991).

Easy bruising

Some children seem to bruise very easily, and because of the high pain threshold mentioned above, may be unable to say how the bruise came about. This has implications for allegations of physical abuse, and careful monitoring of the child's activities and environment should be undertaken in order to see how the bruising is happening if this is a worry.

Lack of vomiting

Many children with PWS rarely vomit, if at all. This is probably caused by the low muscle tone. Thus, if vomiting occurs in those who rarely vomit, it may be a sign of very serious illness, and medical attention should be sought immediately. The lack of vomiting also has implications if the child has eaten something poisonous, has a stomach infection or illness affecting the digestive system. Again, medical treatment should be sought immediately.

Additional physical disabilities

Most children with PWS are generally healthy, although some younger children may be prone to bronchial, asthmatic and chest complaints. However, many also have additional physical disabilities, some of which can be related to PWS, but not all. Some of the main ones are given here.

Not every child has every disability, and some may have none, or be very mildly affected.

Visual impairments

A squint in one or both eyes is extremely common. It is usually correctable by patching or minor surgery whilst the child is very young. Myopia (shortsightedness) is also relatively common. Cases of nystagmus (involuntary and jerky repetitive movement of the eyeballs) have also been reported. An ophthalmological study currently underway has identified several cases where there is a loss of stereo-scopic vision, which can cause difficulties with estimating speed and distance.

Curvature of the spine (scoliosis, lordosis, kyphosis)

Scoliosis is the most common curvature of the spine which occurs in PWS, although other types such as lordosis and kyphosis do occur. Onset may sometimes be very early in life, but can occur at any time during the growing period. It is often possible to treat the curvature with a body brace or splint, but some individuals need major surgery to put a rod into the spine. It appears to be much more common in PWS than in the general population.

Skin problems

Various skin problems can occur with PWS, eczema being relatively common. Cellulitis is a real risk in those who are overweight, and will require medical attention.

Immature sexual development and delayed puberty

This is common in both girls and boys, but varies considerably from one individual to another. Early puberty has been noticed in some girls, but full sexual development is extremely rare. This may mean that boys' voices do not break, facial and pubic hair is very scanty, and the genitals are very small. Undescended testes are very common in boys and can sometimes be brought down by surgical means. The penis is often very small. Girls may not menstruate until their late teens or early twenties (if at all). Breast development may not fully occur. Sexual development can be helped with sex hormones (oestrogen for women and testosterone for men), but should only be carried out after discussions with an endocrinological consultant.

Until very recently, it was believed that both men and women with PWS were sterile and unable to have children. However, it is now known that a woman in Denmark with the syndrome has had a baby. Unfortunately the baby had Angelman syndrome. This is due to the genetics involved in PWS. It had always been theorised that a woman with the deletion-type PWS would have a 50/50 chance of having a child with Angelman syndrome – this case sadly proved the theorists right.

Because the youngster with PWS develops differently to everyone else, sex education needs to be handled very sensitively (see also Chapter 6).

Dental and oral problems

Sticky or thick saliva is very common in PWS, and can be seen as 'crusting' at the corners of the mouth. Tooth enamel is often poor and may be more quickly eroded away. Sometimes this is exacerbated by grinding the teeth or rumination. A high palate is common. Many children have a small jaw, which leads to overcrowding of the teeth. Early dental intervention and subsequent frequent check ups are essential.

Diabetes

Diabetes can occur, although it is relatively rare in children. It is normally associated with significant obesity and is usually Type II. It is more common in adolescents and adults.

Speech and language problems

Speech and language disorders are fairly common in PWS, not just in children but in adults as well. There is quite a range in the type and severity of the disorders, which are discussed more fully in Chapter 2.

Psychological and behavioural characteristics

Much interest has been shown recently by researchers in demonstrating that PWS has a definite behavioural phenotype which may have a genetic basis. Dykens and Kasari (1997) found that certain behaviours were more common in people with PWS than in other types of learning disability. These included: tantrums, skin-picking, arguing a lot, obessions, impulsivity, speech problems, talking too much and underactivity.

Another study carried out by Curfs *et al.* (1995) compared youngsters with PWS with youngsters attending regular schools in The Netherlands. They found that the youngsters with PWS were perceived by their parents as less physically active, less open to new ideas and experiences, less conscientious in task situations, more irritable and immature, and more dependent on other persons. Perhaps surprisingly, they found no difference between the groups in extroversion and emotional stability. They did note 'a great variety of personality-related problems' and proposed that further studies should try to discover how factors in the children's families affected their personalities.

Further research in the Netherlands by van Lieshout *et al.* (1998) suggested that early diagnosis and early parental guidance programmes seem to lower problem behaviours in children with PWS. Additionally, Dykens and Cassidy (1995) found that older children may be at risk from negative self-evaluation, withdrawal and depression, and suggest that this may be because of the child's perception of his or her own vulnerabilities. Thus teachers in nursery and primary schools have a very important role to play in the later development of the child with PWS by helping with behavioural management programmes, and teachers in secondary school and further education can help by providing interventions to improve self-esteem and facilitate successful peer interactions.

The fact that the characteristics of PWS can be exacerbated or tempered by the social environment is underlined by an interesting study which compared Japanese and American children (Hanchett *et al.* 1992). There was a higher incidence in the Americans in the amount of obesity, skin-picking, speech problems and behaviour problems.

However, it must be emphasised again that behaviours vary considerably between individuals, and may lessen or increase over time as well as according to management and other external factors.

Temper outbursts (tantrums)

Temper outbursts in PWS appear to be very common, being reminiscent of the behaviour of a two to three year old child, no matter what the age of the person with PWS. Some individuals rarely have temper outbursts, but at the other end of the scale, there are others whose outbursts are frequent, extremely violent and unpredictable. Most lie somewhere between these two extremes. The most common triggers for outbursts are: being denied food or some other desired item; changes in routine; confusion about a current situation.

Stubbornness

Stubbornness is often linked to a desire to keep to a routine, but at other times there is a complete refusal to comply with instructions or with the rest of the class for no apparent reason. There often is a very valid reason for the child with PWS, but they may find it difficult to articulate, and only the most patient questioning can reveal it. Temper outbursts are likely to occur before a reason is ever arrived at, unless appropriate measures are taken.

Resistance to change

Some observers have remarked that children with PWS show autistic tendencies, and the liking for, if not insistence on, routine certainly reveals some similarities. Whilst some children cope with change relatively easily, others have real difficulties in adjusting to even the slightest variation to routine, particularly when this involves meal times.

Obsessive and/or compulsive behaviour

Obsessive or compulsive behaviour has been demonstrated to affect up to 80 per cent of people with PWS, increasing in number of symptoms with age. Recent research in the USA found examples such as the woman who 'ripped out her knitting and started all over again after making

9

small, correctable mistakes' and 'individuals who routinely missed the school bus or arrived late to work because of excessive time spent tying shoes 'just right' or arranging or re-arranging books in a back-pack.' (Dykens *et al*. 1996).

Hoarding and possessiveness

Hoarding items or being unwilling to share them is relatively common in PWS, and has been linked to obsessive–compulsive aspects of the syndrome. Others have speculated that the behaviour is typical of an individual for whom some aspect of life is beyond their personal control (i.e. food). It manifests in various ways, from just collecting certain items and toys, much as other children do, to collecting more unusual objects such as advertising brochures or pieces of paper. Some children are so possessive of their 'hoard' that they become very agitated if someone tries to take it away from them. A few will steal items from other children to add to their hoard.

Perseveration

Perseveration or persistent talking or questioning on one topic, is another common difficulty. Researchers are not sure whether it has a behavioural or a neurological basis. It can become worse if the child is anxious or confused.

Skin-picking or spot-picking

A form of behaviour which is prevalent in PWS, and unlike any seen in any other syndrome, is so-called 'skin-picking'. It is more severe in some youngsters than others. A few do not have this behaviour, while many develop it after the age of about ten years. Skin-picking initially starts with the youngster picking or scratching at an existing spot or wound. It often spreads to behaviours whereby the youngster deliberately provokes a wound by repeatedly picking or scratching a certain area of the body. It can become so persistent that the wound is never allowed to heal, with all the attendant risks of infection and blood-poisoning.

Immature social skills

Most children with PWS seem to exhibit some difficulties with social skills such as turn-taking and taking part in group activities. A few exhibit behaviours which fall within the autistic spectrum, such as being very isolationist, or finding it difficult to make eye contact. Some children are very friendly and sociable, others can be very introverted; most are egocentric, experiencing problems in appreciating another's point of view or situation.

Mental health problems

Mental health problems in children under 13 are rare, but some challenging behaviour may be so extreme that it could be classed as a mental health problem which may require treatment from a psychiatrist

In teenagers and adults there is some risk of mental health problems developing, notably depression, anxiety, obsessive–compusive disorder, psychosis and schizophrenia. Research into this area of PWS is in its very early stages, but early indications are that mental health problems are more common in PWS than in the general population. Some researchers have noted a cyclical feature to these problems both in depression (Watanabe *et al*. 1997) and in psychosis (Clarke *et al*. 1995).

Speculation remains as to whether mental health problems stem from the physical dysfunctions inherent in PWS or whether they are related to environmental factors such as being treated differently to everyone else with regard to food, or low self-esteem which in turn arises from obesity and physical or intellectual disability.

Drug treatment for mental health problems needs careful monitoring. Some people with PWS have adverse reactions to these types of drug.

Summary

As can be seen from this introduction, Prader-Willi Syndrome is a very complex disorder which requires careful management to enable the individual to remain both healthy and happy, as well as to reach their full potential. A good understanding of the underlying causes of the syndrome can help in devising strategies and techniques to help the child progress. It is important that the child is not seen as lazy, greedy and deceitful, and that their behaviours are not automatically interpreted as the result of bad parenting. Living with a child with PWS can be very stressful for all concerned, but with the right environment and support the child can develop very successfully.

Chapter 2

Cognition

Individuals with PWS vary widely in their abilities. Most are within the MLD range, with a minority having severe learning difficulties, and another minority with the intellectual capability to pass GCSE exams. To date, no evidence has been found at either the genetic or the social level to account for this wide 'scatter' of abilities. However, even those at the higher end of the range often do not perform up to their tested level of ability because of developmental delay at an emotional and social level.

Ability levels

The educational settings in which children with PWS are found reflect this variation. Table 2.1 contains data provided by responses from 101 teachers to a questionnaire carried out by the PWSA (UK) in 1998. Although the sample is small, and is likely to be biased (see Preface), the data are very similar to those provided by previous questionnaires circulated to parents (Waters 1991). There appears to be a gradual shift from mainstream to special needs schools as the child gets older, with a minority remaining within mainstream throughout their school career, usually with classroom support. This may partly reflect not so much the intellectual ability of the pupil, as the fact that as they get older they find it increasingly difficult to cope with the subtleties and complications of teenage and adult life. Behavioural difficulties may also become more apparent as the individual reaches the teenage years. Some experts have linked this with the delayed puberty which often accompanies the syndrome.

Table 2.2 shows the pupils' level of ability as described by teachers, and is also indicative of the wide range of abilities present in PWS. It is thus very difficult to be prescriptive about teaching methods for particular subjects. It is essential that each pupil is assessed as an individual, regardless of the PWS diagnosis, and that methods are used which are appropriate to their level of understanding. Where teachers have taught more than one pupil with PWS, they have reported signficant differences in the personality and abilities of each child. One case was reported of a brother and sister with PWS in the same family, which is very rare. However, even here, one sibling had a more severe speech problem than the other, and the other had a more severe weight problem (Waters 1991).

No. of children/students	11	28	22	29	11
Age range	Under 5 yrs	5–7yrs	8–11yrs	12–16yrs	17+
Type of school	%				
Playgroup + home visit	9%	-	-	-	-
Mainstream nursery	46%	7%	-	-	-
Mainstream primary		39%	37%	-	
Special unit in		14%	14%	-	
Mainstream secondary	-	-	-	6%	9%
Mainstream middle school	-	-	-	3%	-
Physical primary	-	4%	4%	-	-
Physical disabilities and emotionally vulnerable secondary	-	-	-	6%	-
Special needs nursery MLD or mixed	36%	-	-	-	-
Special needs primary, MLD or mixed	-	18%	37%	-	-
Special needs secondary, MLD or mixed		-	4%	75%	36%
Special needs nursery SLD	9%	-	-	-	-
Special needs primary SLD	-	18%	4%		
Special needs secondary SLD	-	-	-	10%	18%
FE College special needs course	-	-	-	-	36%
% with statement or in process	82%	86%	100%	100%	n/a
% in residential school/college	0%	0%	0%	11%	11%

Table 2.1 Age of child with PWS and type of school (from 101 responses to a questionnaire to teachers, PWSA (UK) 1998).

Strengths and weaknesses

Table 2.3 shows the most common strengths and weaknesses of youngsters with PWS as described in the PWSA (UK) 1998 questionnaire to teachers. The strengths and weaknesses listed in the table are those which were most frequently mentioned throughout the age groups (with the most frequent being at the top of each list, descending to the least frequent). There were many others, which are provided in more detail in the chapters relating to each age group. As can be seen from the table, some characteristics which are strengths for some people are weaknesses

No of children/students	11	28	22	29	11
Age range	Under 5	5–7yrs	8–11yrs	12–16yrs	16+
Ability level	%				
Too young to assess/not stated	9%	4%	9%	3%	-
Average	-	4%	-	3%	-
Low average to average	-	4%	5%	7%	-
Mild learning difficulties	27%	7%	9%	7%	18%
Mild to moderate difficulties	-	7%	5%	3%	-
Moderate learning difficulties	46%	46%	58%	40%	64%
Moderate to severere learning difficulties	9%	11%	5%	21%	9%
Severe learning difficulties	9%	17%	9%	13%	9%
Profound and complex learning difficulties	-	-	-	3%	-

Table 2.2 Ages and ability levels of 101 children/students with PWS (as described by teachers in a questionnaire circulated by the PWSA (UK) 1998).

for others (e.g. ability to concentrate, social skills, reading, numeracy). It is thus becomes clear that children and students with PWS can vary considerably in many ways, and each must be treated as an individual.

Research into cognitive profiles in PWS

Some research has been carried out on the cognitive profiles of children with PWS outside of the UK, which broadly reiterates the findings above.

Curfs *et al.* (1991) looked at 26 youngsters with PWS between the ages of seven and fifteen, and found IQ scores ranged from 39–96, with a mean IQ of 62.3, but no clear pattern of cognitive weaknesses, with strengths being more visible. Children scored better on visual motor discrimination skills than on auditory verbal processing skills. A slightly earlier study by Borghgraef *et al.* (1990) gave similar results with IQs ranging betweeen 45 and 95. In three cases, verbal IQ was more than 15 IQ scores higher than the performantial IQ. Taylor (1988) reports isolated cases of IQs over 100.

Dykens *et al.* (1992) found clear patterns of strengths and weaknesses in the cognitive processing and academic achievements of persons with PWS. Weaknesses were identified in sequential processing relative to simultaneous processing and achievements. Consequently, there may be difficulties with short term memory and with processing information in a step-by-step manner, but strengths lay in 'the integration of stimuli in a spatial mode'.

One of the earliest studies into cognitive processing in PWS was

Strengths	Weaknesses
Under 9 years	**Under 9 years**
Friendly and sociable with peers and adults	Stubbornness, obstinacy
Determined to succeed	Handwriting, pencil skills
Independent	Expressive speech
Good sense of humour	Short attention span
Good concentration	Temper tantrums/outbursts
Reading	Obsessiveness
Good memory	Lack of adaptability, difficulty adjusting to new ideas
Communication skills	Poor relationship with peer group
9–13 years	**9–13 years**
Reading	Short attention span
Determination	Numeracy
Sociable with peers	Stubbornness, obstinacy
Good sense of humour	Writing
Kind/caring/loving	Reading
Sociable with adults	Emotionally immature
Good general knowledge and interest in world around	Obsessive
Likes to be helpful/take messages	Lack of adaptability, difficulty adjusting to new ideas
14+ years	**14+ years**
Determination	Immature socially and emotionally
Art	Numeracy
Sociable with peers and adults	Stubbornness, obstinacy
Reading	Lack of adaptability, difficulty adjusting to change
Good sense of humour	Short attention span
Likes to be helpful/take messages	Reading
Kind, caring	
Numeracy	Temper tantrums/outbursts

Table 2.3 Strengths and weaknesses as described by 101 teachers in a questionnaire carried out by the PWS (UK) 1998. Characteristics are listed in order of most frequently mentioned.

carried out by Gabel *et al.* (1986). 15 children with a mean age of 12.4 years were matched with 15 controls of 'normal home-dwelling children' for age and sex with a mean age of 11.93 years. The Prader-Willi subjects obtained a mean mental age equivalent score of 4.14 on auditory attention tests and 7.64 years on visual attention tests. The control group scored 9.98 for the auditory attention test and 11.02 for the visual attention tests, thus indicating that for the PW group, auditory attention is on average greater than three years lower than visual tests, as compared with a one year discrepancy in the control group. This pattern has been reproduced in later studies.

The relationship between intellectual ability and behaviour

Contrary to what might be supposed, there has been little evidence to support the theory that the more able the child, the less problematic their behaviour is likely to be. Dykens and Cassidy (1995) report that 'high IQ does not seem a protective factor against significant behavioral problems in Prader-Willi syndrome'.

Curfs *et al.* (1991) originally found no relation between behaviour problems, gender and IQ, but in a later study (Curfs *et al.* 1995), the researchers found that girls scored lower on emotional stability, and that youngsters with higher IQs were more extrovert and physically active.

The relationship between intellectual ability and obesity

An early study by Crnic *et al.* (1980) proposed that IQ diminished as weight increased, but this was not found to be the case by Dykens *et al.* (1992). They theorised that the ability to access food might be a more critical variable in obesity, and that those functioning at higher levels may be at greater risk of obesity as they could be more resourceful, active or ingenious about obtaining food.

Many children and young adolescents can be extremely knowledgeable about their dietary requirements but find theory and practice very difficult to reconcile. A typical case was the young woman who told guests at a Christmas meal that she could only have boiled potatoes, and helped herself to the correct amount. She was later discovered eating the roast potato leftovers from the waste bin.

The relationship between intellectual ability and age

James and Brown (1992) found evidence of a performance decline as the child got older, but at the same Dykens found nothing to support this theory (Dykens *et al.* 1992). This requires further reseach, and one author has suggested that it is the gap between the performance of the child with PWS and that of his or her peers which gets larger, not that the child starts to decline as an individual (Taylor 1988).

Speech and language disorders appear to be very common, both in girls and boys. In the questionnaire to teachers, 71 per cent of under eight year olds and 40 per cent of over eight year olds were described as having some some sort of language delay or disorder. Some children known to the author have attended schools specifically for children with speech and language disorders. There is no common type of disorder.

Speech and language disorders

Akefeldt *et al.* (1997) studied 11 individuals with PWS aged between four and 25 years, comparing them with 11 non-PWS individuals of the same sex, age, body mass index and IQ level. The researchers found that seven out of eight children aged eight years or older had difficulties in oral motor abilities as well as a high pitch level. They also noted impaired abilities in grammar, phonology and comprehension.

An earlier study by Kleppe *et al.* (1990) of 18 children between the ages of eight and 17 provided many details of the type of speech and language characteristics they found. Overall intelligibility was judged to be below average for every subject, and all 18 exhibited at least one consonant error, with 15 exhibiting three or more consonant errors. All had some difficulties with rapidly alternating speech movements. Fluency was problematic in most cases, but only one individual was considered to be a stutterer. Word-recall difficulties could account for disfluencies such as interjections, revisions, repetitions, and incomplete phrases. None of the children in Kleppe's study had major hearing difficulties which were likely to contribute to speech problems, but the PWSA (UK) is aware of a few children with PWS who do have hearing impairments. A study in New Zealand suggested those with hearing impairments were more likely to have atypical PWS (Personal correspondence).

This study also found that, with one exception, all subjects scored well below their chronological age for receptive language, and this discrepancy increased with age. For 15 of the subjects expressive language was also below chronological age, but they scored higher on vocabulary tests. Signficantly different profiles were recorded between individuals, indicating the need for individual therapies and programmes for each child.

Whyte (1998), who is a speech and language therapist in the UK, has made personal observations from her own caseload of children with PWS. She suggests that delayed speech development may be due more to hypotonia and consequent inability to produce accurate articulation, rather than to a specific language delay. Other observations made by Whyte are:

- inability to elevate the tongue tip is common and complicated by a high-arched narrow palate;
- flaccid dysarthria may be present due to weak muscle tone (i.e. inaccuracy of movements and inability to change from one tongue or lip position to another);
- dyspraxia is occasionally present, and the incidence of this may be higher than in the rest of the population;
- weak voice, owing to bilateral vocal fold flaccidity;
- high pitched voice, which may not change in boys in puberty (may be helped with hormone treatment);
- hypernasality.

In the USA, Downey and Knutson (1995) report that, generally speaking, expressive language is more significantly impaired than receptive language. There are undoubtedly exceptions to this, with children exhibiting very good articulation and vocabulary skills, but with little understanding of what they are saying.

A very specific individual programme of speech therapy should therefore be in place for the child with PWS who exhibits difficulties in this area, and should be included within the child's Statement of Need (Record of Needs in Scotland).

Specific learning difficulties associated with PWS

While it is important to remember that each child is an individual, there remain several characteristics which seem to be common to many children with PWS though they are present to a greater degree in some than in others. A summary of these follows:

Difficulty with auditory processing

A child may find it difficult to understand verbal instructions, or to cope with too many instructions at once, necessitating the breaking down of instructions into small steps and providing additional pictorial cues.

Perseveration

Asking a question again and again or reverting to the same topic is very common. Experts are still unsure if this is a linguistic or behavioural problem or both.

Difficulties with abstract concepts, especially number and time

Confusion over time concepts can be problematic, and may continue into adulthood. Temporal meanings such as 'before', 'after', 'until' may be confused, and this has implications for narrative speech and writing, as well as grammar.

Difficulties with problem-solving strategies and consequent stubbornness

Following on from the problems of time and sequential processing come difficulties with problem solving. The logical steps of 'first I do this, and then I do this' can be difficult to grasp for the child with PWS, and the resulting confusion can exacerbate stubborn refusals to move on from the first step.

Rigid thinking, difficulties with re-assessing what has been learned

What is learned, if not forgotten, will be difficult to 'unlearn', so that new methods of approach can result in argument, e.g. 'You told me to do it this way'. Two American authors sum this up neatly:

Attempting to explain an issue to persons with PWS who have already an established mind set usually reveals concrete thinking, lack of capacity to abstract or follow a chain of logic, inability to learn from experience, inability to shift perspective, or alter a preset train of thought. Failure to learn from experience may explain why traditional behavior modification programs have only limited success   (Whitman and Greenswag 1995).

Poor short-term memory, but good long-term memory

A topic learned one day may have been forgotten by the next, so that repetition in a number of situations is essential. On the other hand, long-term memory, especially for places, people, events and meals, is very good.

Difficulties with applying methods

Although methods of doing a task can be learned by rote, the child may still have difficulties understanding how to apply them. Thus, the child may apply a single rule to all situations or, conversely, be unable to see how a rule used in one situation can also be used in another. This is particularly the case with mathematics and science.

Summary

Children with PWS tend to work best in an environment which offers them as little anxiety as possible. Conflicts, dissension, or opposing viewpoints can be very confusing for them. It is essential therefore that the following features are built into the school environment for the child with PWS, even more than for most children:

- clear guidelines and rules for the whole school/class which are visibly displayed;
- clear expectations of rewards and, usually less necessary, loss of privileges for good/bad behaviour;
- a consistent approach to undesired behaviour from all staff. It is confusing for the child if one staff member makes him leave the room if his behaviour is difficult while another sits him down in a corner and tries to talk it through with him;
- the involvement of all staff, including auxiliaries, caretakers, dinner supervisors, taxi drivers and escorts in the consistent approach, particularly with regard to access to food;
- the use of visual prompts, lists, and written or pictorial instructions to convey important messages and to enforce instructions;
- a step by step approach to learning.

Chapter 3
Preschool and Primary Age Children: Classroom and Behaviour Management

Preschool children with PWS are usually very loving, and seem to make friends wherever they go. Like other children, very young children with PWS generally benefit from associating with other children of the same age. In fact, in many respects, early nursery or play group education is absolutely vital to provide a good start to their lives. It can help in many areas where children with PWS often have difficulties, such as learning social skills and developing gross and fine motor skills.

Dietary needs and supervision

Many teachers and parents report that they have few problems with eating in very young children. Some may still experience difficulty chewing because of poor muscle tone in the facial muscles. In most cases they quite readily accept whatever is given to them, and will generally be happy with a piece of fruit rather than a biscuit. However, they may take the opportunity to help themselves to various semi-edible items which are found in the classroom environment e.g. playdough, pet food, dried pasta shapes etc. Thus, careful monitoring of the child needs to be undertaken, especially when they first enter nursery, to ensure that they do not have these propensities. Simple rules of healthy eating can also be taught to the whole class.

Liaison with parents is very important. Some children may already have a break between meals of a piece of fruit or plain biscuit built into their dietary regime, perhaps with a drink of low calorie squash or semi-skimmed milk; others may not be allowed breaks because they have larger portions at main meals. Generally speaking, if other children in the class are having a break, there may be fewer difficulties if the child with PWS also has one, but of a low calorie variety.

Ancillary staff such as caretakers, cleaners, dinner supervisors, taxi escorts etc. all need to be advised not to give sweets or biscuits to the child with PWS. If the child is spending all day at the nursery, lunchtime meals need to be discussed with the parents – a packed lunch may be a better option than prepared school meals.

Social skills

Children of this age tend to be very friendly towards everyone. They are usually very placid, happy and loving, the occasional tantrum excepted.

The preschool child with PWS

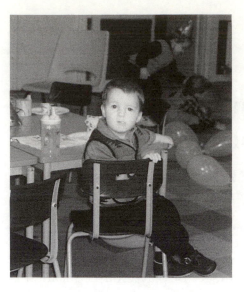

Figure 3.1 A three year old boy at a nursery party

As they are likely to be smaller than the rest of the group, other children may try to 'mother' them. Sharing and turn taking can be problematic, and if this is the case, there should be a lot of input into helping them to overcome these difficulties. This is not something they will grow out of without considerable intervention at an early age, and the more it is addressed at this stage, the easier it becomes later on.

Small group work is an important aspect of the child's development, but one to one with a teacher or teaching aide may be necessary when working on new concepts, or tasks the child finds difficult. Generally speaking, children with PWS work best in a one to one situation, but a few may find it stressful and pressurising to be the sole focus of attention.

Tiredness

All people with PWS seem to need more sleep than most, and very young children will often need an afternoon nap. Like most children, they will quickly become irritable and unable to concentrate if they are tired.

Routine

Many young children with PWS like to have a set routine to their day, and some may become very distressed by changes to that routine. It is important at this early stage in life to introduce elements of change and simple choice whenever possible, but not to do so in a complicated or confusing way. A child who consistently chooses the same colour to use, or the same book to look at, could be given two other colours or books and asked to choose between them. Others can become anxious or confused about what will happen each day. A simple pictorial timetable pinned in a prominent place can help with this. Sometimes if a more than usual change of routine is planned, or occurs unexpectedly, the child with PWS will require one to one input to internalise the idea.

Bringing a 'cueing' object to a new lesson can also help the transition between one subject and another, or between rooms e.g. bringing a ball to a PE lesson.

Toileting skills

Children with PWS vary considerably as to the time they become independent with regard to toileting. A few will be able to take themselves to the toilet as young as three or four, others will need help for much longer. There can be a tendency to ask to go to the toilet if they are not enjoying the lesson, or want the attention of a particular member of staff. Others may spend a long time ostensibly just sitting on the toilet, or even falling asleep. All of these behaviours can be discouraged by making it clear at the outset how much time can be spent at the toilet.

Dietary needs and supervision

Infants

Like preschool children, most young children of primary school age tend to accept the need for dietary control, especially if they have been diagnosed with PWS at a young age and have become used to the regime. Sometimes a diagnosis may be made at around this age, and this can be more difficult for both the child and the parents if the parents have become used to giving in to the child's demands for food. Even at five years old, the child can be considerably overweight – cases of children weighing seven stone have been recorded.

Another possible difficulty for the school can become apparent at this stage. Some parents are unwilling or unable to implement dietary controls at home, and this can cause conflict and confusion for the child if the teaching staff are trying to educate him or her about healthy eating. It cannot be said too often that a child with PWS needs to be treated in the same way by everyone in their lives; otherwise they become confused and anxious, or may become manipulative, playing one party off against another. This is obviously a delicate issue for the school to handle, and there may be justifiable concerns about being too judgemental about parents. However, it is in the child's best interests if everyone can agree a suitable dietary regime, and if possible, call an informal meeting with the parents, and another expert such as a school nurse, community dietitian or paediatrician, or even someone from the PWSA (UK) to discuss how an agreed approach to dietary control can be reached.

Although most children with PWS present few problems with regard to behaviour around food before the age of seven, there have been cases of children who steal food, or become aggressive if they cannot have the food they want. These and other behavioural problems require a firm and structured approach from all concerned. A reward system for good behaviour seems to work better than punishment. At this early age, children are usually content to work

Figure 3.2 First day at school for 4½ year old Rachel

towards stars, smiley faces, house points, badges etc., especially if on attaining their targets they are praised loudly to others. Bear in mind too that children with PWS tend to listen in to other people's conversations. Praising them behind their backs, if you are aware of them 'listening in', can be a very strong incentive. It is important that all staff stick to the same formula, and that the child has a very firm structure to work within.

If possible, introduce exciting, interesting activities in the half hour before meal time to divert the child's attention away from food.

Class parties can usually be managed well by liaising with parents over what the child can have to eat. In some cases, special food will be brought for them, and in others the rule will be 'just a little of what everyone else has'.

Children of this age and younger can readily understand simple rules of healthy eating, such as 'If you eat too much you won't be able to run about', 'Plenty of vegetables will keep you healthy', and these are messages which can often be incorporated into the curriculum.

Social skills

Some children are still playing and working well with others at this stage, but others are beginning to show signs of being unable to handle the give and take which is required within groups, and while other children are beginning to appreciate that others' views and feelings are important, the child with PWS may still be at the 'me first' stage, causing them to be bossy, rude, unable to take turns or share. Strategies for those whose development in this area is signficantly delayed include:

- simple role play;
- group games;
- board games;
- working with older pupils on some tasks;
- liaising with parents to find out if there are local groups such as Brownies or Scouts which the child could attend.

For those who will not share or take turns, reward systems could be tried with points/stars etc. awarded for good behaviour. Always praise when the child makes even the smallest breakthrough in this regard.

Attachment to specific members of staff

A tendency to become obsessed with one teacher or helper can begin to manifest itself at this stage, and may continue throughout life, especially if it is not addressed early on (see also the section of this chapter on junior age children, and Chapter 7). Strategies which may help with this include:

- reward for working with a different helper, staff member or other child;
- timed periods of work with preferred helper (using child's alarm clock or similar), then an agreed expectation that the child will do something else.

Perseveration

Many very young children with PWS have speech and language problems, but some have very well developed speech. Sometimes expressive speech is better than comprehension, so the child will use words and phrases which they do not really understand. Like other children of a slightly younger age, many with PWS will tend to perseverate, i.e. repeat a question over and over again, even when you have given them an answer. There are several methods which might be successfully employed to overcome this:

- if you have already answered the question, ask the child to repeat the answer;
- if it is a certain topic they have fixated on, point to the clock, indicating when the topic must be changed (i.e. no more than five more minutes talking about it);
- give the child a card which displays the answer to their question. For example, if they keep asking, 'Did I do that right?' the card might say, 'I did my sums right today!'.

There are further suggestions in Chapter 5 which may be relevant to this age group.

Play time and breaks

Children with PWS should be encouraged and supported to join in with others' games; some will need little encouragement; others can find social skills very difficult. Although the energy and activity of the playground can be overwhelming for some children, it is important that they get as much exercise as possible within break periods to help with weight control.

Home–school relations

Apart from the dietary concerns, which have already been mentioned, there are other reasons why home–school contact is essential for children with PWS. It is helpful if parents can inform the school if the child has had a disturbed night or has had a tantrum before setting out for school. This will have implications for possible behavioural problems during the day. If an exciting event is upcoming at home, it may be impossible for the child to concentrate on their school tasks. Equally, a child who has had an upset at school may carry this on into home, and the parent needs to know what has happened in order to understand their child's behaviour. Children who are falling asleep a great deal at school may need monitoring at home to check that they are not having disturbed sleep or suffering from sleep apnoea.

The most successful way of maintaining home–school liaison is the 'home–school diary' which should be completed on a daily basis whenever possible. Even much older children will benefit from this type of home–school liaison. Suggested topics for inclusion are:

- details of extra treats or parties which have happened at school;
- unusual events at home or school;
- signs of illness, even if only slight;
- unusual sleepiness;
- upsurges in behavioural difficulties;
- details of work well done or behaviour which has exceeded expectations.

Outings

These should cause few problems, as most children with PWS enjoy the prospect of an outing (provided they are well-prepared for it in advance), and will usually stay close to the adult in charge. If pocket-money is allowed, someone should be with the child in the shop to ensure that the money is spent on a non-edible item. Outings which involve long walks are not usually on the agenda for primary children anyway, but be aware that steep hills and long periods standing can be very wearing for children with PWS and they will become tired before most of the other children, with all the possible ensuing behavioural problems such as tantrums and stubborn behaviour.

Juniors

There is often a dilemma at this stage in the child's education as to whether they should remain in mainstream or transfer to a special school. Some children with PWS cope relatively well in the mainstream junior school environment, but sometimes need to repeat Year 2 before progressing to junior school. However, there may be others whose needs would be better met within the special school environment, and it is probably better to transfer them at the beginning of their time at junior school than later on, so as to provide minimal disruption and confusion to the child.

Dietary needs and supervision

The interest in food may become more apparent as the child gets older, and this can become very problematic for some. However, others are still very accepting of the need to keep to a low calorie diet, and will inform strangers, other children and new staff about their needs. Those who find it difficult to keep to their diet will need extra support and environmental controls. This may mean:

- supervision during play times;
- supervision during lunch;
- all lunch boxes locked away;
- encouragement of healthy eating for all;
- warning all ancillary staff about the child's needs;
- putting semi-edible foods such as pet food out of reach;
- keeping money locked away.

If parents/carers agree, it should also be possible in some cases to introduce an element of choice into diet, so that some control is given back to the child. For instance at parties, the child might be offered the choice between a piece of birthday cake and a pudding at lunchtime, or half a piece of birthday cake and half the usual portion of pudding. However, this needs to be introduced carefully, as some children will find even this simple decision beyond them – others will quite happily make the desired choice.

If food is stolen, it is best not to make a big issue out of it. Do not rebuke the child in front of the rest of the class, but take the child to one side and discuss the situation with them. Whilst it can be explained to the child that stealing is wrong and may result in loss of privileges, it can also be helpful to give them a way to take charge of the situation, e.g. by suggesting they do a Wordsearch or puzzle if they are getting hungry, or if they are waiting for others to finish. It is very important to praise the child if they subsequently do not take food if they have access to it.

Pica (eating non-food items) is known in PWS, but is not as common as might be thought. Little research has been done on this subject, but anecdotally parents have reported their children eating items such as soap, toothpaste, sponges, fluff off clothing, paper and, occasionally, faeces.

By this age, a child with PWS can show a very great awareness of their dietary needs. One 11 year old child described herself thus in a talk she gave to her class (her own spellings are retained in the script):

I could wish I didn't have this Syndrom because I have to be on a special diet which makes me diffrent from everybody else. Also I am not allowed to take sweets from other people except my mum or dad or from my teachers or if everyone elese gets I am allowed to have half a packet. I find it hard to keep to my diet allmost all the time because if I didn't I would end up in hospital, very ill indeed. I eat mostly fruite and vegetables becasue thier the right healthay foods. I get biscuits akasonallay now and again once in a while . . . (Waters 1993).

Social skills

The remarks made in the previous sections for younger primary age children also apply here, although the gap in social skills between some children with PWS and their peers may be even more evident now. Some researchers are now speculating that some people with PWS are within the autistic spectrum, and if this is the case, then strategies used for children with autism may be appropriate for the child with PWS. On the other hand, there are many children of this age who play and work well with others, and are well accepted.

School assemblies and other gatherings

Occasionally, either because of immature social skills or a language disorder, the child with PWS may not appreciate that they should remain quiet during school assemblies and formal gatherings. They may shout out a response to something that has been said, or start talking about a topic which has just come into their head. Probably the best way to deal with this is to ensure that the child is always seated near the end of the row so that they can be quietly removed from the assembly by a teacher or assistant. Once they have had their say – out of earshot of the rest of the school – they may be quite willing to return and sit quietly. Children who persist with this could be offered a reward (e.g. a favourite activity) if they remain quiet.

Special occasions and festivals

Christmas and Easter time are particularly trying for the child with PWS, as other children may be talking about the sweets and chocolate they are expecting. Most families will give their child only one chocolate egg at Easter, preferring to give other non-edible gifts as well. Teachers should be aware of these additional strains on children.

The run-up to the Christmas holidays can also be a difficult time. There are disruptions to the usual school routine with rehearsals for school plays, the plays themselves, and parties, as well as the excitement of Christmas around the corner. Added to this is the fact that the autumn term is often quite long, and the child may well be getting very tired with school work. All these factors need to be taken into account if a child's behaviour begins to worsen around this time.

Harvest time is also problematic. The mother of one girl with PWS who had a particularly severe appetite problem told how the harvest display of food was mounted in the classroom for a whole week before the actual festival. Eventually the girl could stand the temptation no longer, and she took and ate some of the food. She was severely reprimanded for this, which in itself was somewhat harsh, but with a little forethought and better understanding, the whole situation could have been avoided.

Concept of time

Many youngsters' concept of time is still very immature at this age. The idea of 'tomorrow', 'next week' or 'next month' may be almost meaningless. It is important then that future events are not flagged up too far in advance, otherwise perseveration and anxiety set in.

Emotional outbursts, crying, screaming, or tantrums

Tantrums or temper outbursts would probably have been tolerated as fairly typical of their age group when the child was in preschool or nursery class. However, children with PWS go on to have difficulties controlling their emotions throughout their lives, and this may begin to become more evident as the child gets older and goes into the higher primary classes. Emotional development on all levels appears delayed to a greater or lesser extent in all children with PWS, and it can be unhelpful to expect them to 'act their age' when they find this very difficult. While it is impossible to avoid every emotional outburst, it is possible to manage the child's environment to some extent to minimise the risk. This would include:

- clear explanations of tasks;
- clear expectations of outcomes and limits;
- unpressured tasks;
- quiet environment for difficult tasks;
- removal of any food from the vicinity;
- praising the child when they have not had an outburst where one might have been expected;
- insistence on class rules (displayed in a prominent place) for all children;
- consistent approach to outbursts (e.g. removal from room, removal of privileges) for all children and from all staff.

Most outbursts have 'triggers', although in some cases it may be difficult to identify them. For instance, a child may become unusually distracted or more volatile at a certain time of day. Closer monitoring may reveal that an ice-cream van is parked in view of the school windows at that time, and measures may need to be taken to ensure the child is working out of sight of the van. Some of the more common 'triggers' of outbursts are:

- change of routine;
- a dispute with another child which the child with PWS does not have the social skills to negotiate;
- tiredness;
- presence of food nearby, or proximity to meal time;
- not wishing to take part in an activity.

The management of tantrums is similar to that which would be used for a younger child:

- remove the child from the scene of the outburst, if possible, or
- remove the audience;
- stay very calm and talk softly;
- use humour;
- get someone else to take over if you are the object of the outburst;
- do not attempt to reason with the child;
- do not get into an argument with them;
- do not take a confrontational approach;
- do not give in to their demands;
- distract their attention if possible;
- once the tantrum is over, give the child time to regain their equilibrium. This may mean allowing them a quiet time on their own, or even a short nap;
- talk about what happened later on, and discuss what can be done to help prevent it happening again;
- have clear expectations of behaviour which apply to the whole class.

There are sometimes signs that the child is about to lose control, which only close observation of the child over a period of time would reveal. However, if the signs are recognised, it is sometimes possible to avoid an outburst by distracting attention or intervening at an early stage.

Stubborn or obstinate behaviour

This is quite common in children with PWS, and probably stems from the difficulties they have in adapting to change or new ideas. Sometimes it may result from a genuine difficulty which the child is unable to verbalise. However, they can often be helped to overcome this. The following are suggestions which may help:

- reward for cooperation (favourite activity if current task is completed, stars, badges etc.);
- give other children who have finished their work activities which the child with PWS will also want to do, pointing out that 'as they have finished, they can do this now . . .'.
- ignore for a while if the behaviour appears to be attention-seeking.

Obsessive behaviour

Although obsessive behaviour tends to be more problematic with the older age groups, it can become apparent at a very early age, and wherever possible, suitable interventions should be devised to prevent it, especially where the behaviour is becoming disruptive to the teacher, the child, or other pupils. However, it may be the case that a behaviour has a calming or soothing function for the child, and thus any increase in a particular type of behaviour may be a signal of stress, frustration or anxiety elsewhere in the child's life. Total elimination of a behaviour which the child finds soothing may result in some worse form of behaviour surfacing in the future.

The most common behaviours include: only wanting to use certain pens or pencils, bringing items into class and refusing to be parted from them, drawing or writing patterns or symbols over and over again, picking at skin and clothing, and ritualistic behaviour around certain objects. Others fixate on certain persons, often a teacher or classroom assistant, sometimes another pupil. Some ideas for managing obsessive behaviour include:

- encouraging interaction with others or ask the child to help another child or a staff member to divert attention away from object or person obsessing them;
- role playing how the obsession affects others;
- trying to keep occupied during 'listening activities', especially if skin-picking is problematic – e.g. a ball of wool to wind for teacher or assistant;
- using habits productively – e.g. if the child likes tearing up paper, give them all the waste paper in the class to tear up and dispose of;
- limiting the activity to certain times or places – e.g. just before lunch, in the book corner;
- giving a gentle reminder to move on.

Difficulties adapting to change in routine

If a child has difficulty coping with change, it is essential that there is as much intervention as possible at this stage of the child's life as they will find it even more difficult as they get older. Some suggestions for making changes easier are:

- inform the whole class well in advance of any changes (if possible);
- take time to discuss the implications with the child, and inform parents/carers so that they can provide the same information and a consistent approach, thus preventing the child from becoming even more confused or anxious by conflicting explanations;
- use a calendar to display future events;
- have a visual display of the day's activities on the wall/board. If an activity changes or is switched, allow the child with PWS to make the necessary change to the display;
- present unforeseeable changes as 'a big surprise'.

One advantage of the desire to stick to a routine can be that possibly unpopular tasks such as exercise or cleaning up after artwork are more likely to be complied with if they are always carried out at a particular time of day, or as part of the daily routine.

Taking control

Because it is difficult for children with PWS to control some areas of their lives, it is important that recognition is given to those areas where they can excel. They are often very keen to help the teacher or run simple messages, and can gain a lot of self-esteem by doing these tasks well. However, for some children it should be borne in mind that an errand which takes them past the dining room just before dinner time, or any other place where food is available (e.g. where lunch boxes are stored, or the canteen garbage area) can lead to unnecessary temptation.

Child study by Carolynn Smith

Michael is seven years old and he is in a Year 3 class at a school for pupils with severe learning difficulties. Michael has integrated at a small private school since reception year. He currently attends a small class at the mainstream school for three days a week and comes to the SLD school on Thursdays and Fridays. This combination has been highly successful, and we feel this has helped him to achieve so highly. Very close links are maintained with his other school to ensure total coverage of the National Curriculum. It is hoped that in the future, Michael will attend mainstream school with or without support.

He exhibits some behavioural problems in three key areas:

- Completing a task in a set period of time. Michael works slowly and methodically, and he will not hurry up to finish his work.
- Controlling his own eating. He is fine in controlled situations i.e. when he has his own pre-packed lunch box, but at class parties or school trips he will eat indefinitely. When this is limited by staff, he becomes very upset and says he is still hungry.

- A change in routine. For example, Michael insists that he packs and unpacks his school bag, and that he carries his lunchbox – if this does not happen he becomes very upset.

Michael finds some physical activities difficult but there has been a recent improvement since he had his body brace removed. He will take part in class games for a brief period before opting out and saying he is tired.

Michael's academic abilities are very good. He achieved Level 2C for his reading in the SATs and Level 1 for maths.

Teachers try to be very positive but firm and calm when he becomes upset, and if required move him to a favourite activity, which usually calms him down.

Chapter 4

Preschool and Primary Age Children: Educational Techniques

Children with PWS develop at different rates, and some may arrive at nursery or pre-school classes with significant difficulties in walking and talking. Others will have walked relatively early and/or be incessant chatterers. Many infants with PWS start school in mainstream classes. However, if at the time the child is due to transfer from nursery to infant classes. The child's developmental age is below five, it may be helpful for the child to repeat the last year in nursery class before moving on to infant school. The input of an educational psychologist is very beneficial at this stage.

If the teacher has no experience of teaching children with PWS, it may be possible to find a school in the area which has had pupils with the syndrome, and to arrange for some training in best practice to take place. It is essential that the teacher transfers her knowledge about PWS to any classroom assistants or teacher's aides who may be involved in the care of the child with PWS.

Preschool and infants

The Statement of Need (Record of Needs in Scotland)

Although some children with PWS start school without a Statement of Need, and indeed may be deemed not to require one, most will have one in place within a year or two of starting school. Those who do not have a statement need to be carefully monitored to ensure that they are keeping up with their peers, and any concerns addressed before they become crises.

The statement will of course vary considerably from one individual to another, but almost all will require some one to one or small group input for key subjects. Some will also require speech therapy, physiotherapy or occupational therapy. The statement should also make reference to the need for dietary control.

General abilities and methods of working to produce the best results across the curriculum

Two separate patterns emerged in the questionnaire to teachers carried out by the PWSA (UK). There were children who were able to concentrate, even at a very young age, for very long periods of time on a task they found absorbing, and another group who had many of the symptoms of attention-deficit disorder and could not concentrate at all.

Overall strengths and weaknesses were also very variable, with some features appearing as strengths for some children and weaknesses in others.

Table 4.1 shows the strengths and weaknesses of children aged seven and under as described by teachers in the questionnaire. Of course, not all children will have all the strengths or all the weakness, and all will have individual traits, but the responses are very characteristic of PWS.

Even with the wide variation of characteristics and abilities, there are several methods of working to which most young children with PWS respond best. These include:

- one to one or small group work;
- using visual prompts and signs;
- using Makaton signing to help those with speech and language difficulties;
- use mnenomics and rhymes to aid learning;
- 'helping teacher' by helping another pupil;
- practical activities and concrete, as opposed to abstract, work;
- short tasks;

Strengths	Weaknesses
Happy, friendly nature	Heightened sensitivity to normal classroom environment, easily distracted/upset
Independent	Unable to dress or toilet self
Determined to succeed	Strong-willed/will not accept help
Good communication skills/tries hard to communicate	Speech difficult, below average vocabulary
Good peer relations, sociable	Poor social skills, no close friends
Good memory	Poor short term memory
Good concentration	Overconcentrates/spends long periods on same activity
Sense of humour	Very short attention span
Good computer skills	Obsessiveness
Imaginative play	Repetitive and perseverative speech
Listens and understands well	Listening to instructions
Shows remorse and desire to improve	Poor coordination
Eager to please	Stubborn, argumentative
Reading ability/enjoys books	Reading
Likes to help others	Difficult to share or take turns
Puzzles	Cutting skills
Threading, peg board work	Poor hand control and pencil skills
Colouring	Gross motor performance
Responds well to praise	Difficult to motivate
Logical mind	Unable to adapt to change/difficulty with new ideas
Number work	Number work
Musical ability	Temper tantrums, irrational, aggressive
Good relationship with adults	Dependent on adult help for activities

Table 4.1 Strengths and weaknesses of children with PWS aged seven and under (from a questionnaire to teachers carried out by the PWSA (UK) 1998).

- a reward if a task is finished satisfactorily;
- appealing to competitive nature, e.g. 'I bet you can't . . .';
- allowing time to get thoughts in order and to speak;
- clear, small, step by step instructions;
- asking the child to 'repeat back' instructions to ensure they are understood;
- regular routine, visible timetable (e.g. on board or wall);
- lots of praise;
- clear boundaries;
- initiate new ideas and give most difficult tasks first thing in the morning;
- use tick boxes/multiple choice formats in tests when children have difficulty writing;
- use an easeled work surface to make writing easier and less fatiguing;
- seating arrangements which minimise distraction from others.

Working in larger groups or taking part in class discussions can be overwhelming and confusing for some children with PWS because of their difficulties with auditory processing. They may find it difficult to keep track of what is happening, and thus tend to withdraw from the activity. Large, noisy classes can also be very distracting, requiring more one to one input than a smaller class. Peers with challenging behaviour can also have a very detrimental affect on a young child with PWS. As with all young children, the best work is usually done in the morning, but attention levels may drop as break or lunchtime approaches and the thought of food takes over. Children with PWS tire easily, and most will find it difficult to work in the afternoon; some may find work gets more difficult as the week or term goes on. Routine is also very important, but it should not be allowed to dominate the child's life. Introduce small changes wherever possible, and encourage simple choices.

Many children seem to find imaginative play or putting themselves in someone else's place difficult. Puppets and simple role play can help with this. Children with PWS enjoy role play. John, for instance, responded well to the aeroplane set up in his nursery. He put on his seat belt and said, 'got my money'. He then got up and took the other passengers a cup of tea and a biscuit, saying, 'tea' (see Figure 4.1).

Practical tasks can sometimes be difficult, due to poor muscle tone in the hands, or poor hand–eye coordination. The use of special scissors, play dough, sand etc. can help improve tone and general dexterity. However, children with PWS can demonstrate particular skills with jigsaw puzzles, which many also enjoy. Jigsaws can be used as reward tasks, or as learning aids for colours and shapes.

Much repetitive practise and learning in very small steps is usually required. Some children are over-confident, saying they know how to perform a task even when they don't. In such cases, tasks should be presented in a number of different ways to prevent boredom.

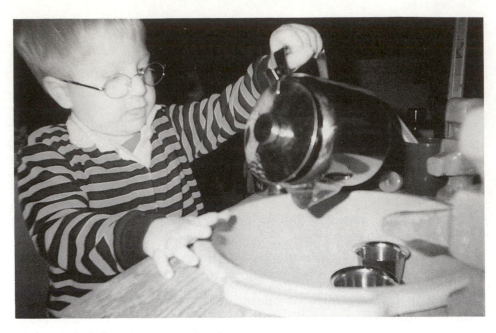

Figure 4.1 John enjoying role play

Literacy skills

Reading and writing ability will depend to a large extent on the degree of learning disability, with some children having few difficulties, and others having clear delays in this area. Sometimes, however, ability can be affected by other factors such as motor control and language problems.

Pencil and hand control may be helped by the use of a sloping board, a thicker pencil, foam tubing over the barrel of the pencil, and using larger pieces of paper. A small step for the feet under the desk can also provide a more comfortable working position, giving additional overall balance. If pencil control is a major problem, consider the use of computers or other electronic aids, as the child may be able to manage these relatively well, and therefore progress overall at a faster rate. Dot to dot, tracing and patterning is also useful for some children. Individual occupational therapy support may also be necessary.

In reading, flash cards could be helpful – there may be a tendency to remember words rather than read them. Constant practise is necessary to ensure that work done one day is not forgotten the next, and each step should be well learned before proceeding to the next.

Numeracy skills

Like reading and writing, numeracy skills will depend to some extent on the extent of the learning disability, but it is generally recognised that, with some exceptions, children with PWS are better at reading and writing than number work. This is probably due to the difficulties involved in processing abstract concepts. Difficulties can also arise when one type of calculation has been well learned, and then the move must be made to another, e.g. switching from addition to subtraction. Even when more than one method is known, the child may still have difficulty choosing the appropriate one for the task. Sorting and matching skills are often relatively good.

Number work should have a very practical basis. Clapping and nursery rhymes can help with learning numbers by rote. Children who can count may still have difficulty appreciating that, say, 2 + 3 always equals 5. Many will insist on counting out the numbers again, for example on their fingers or with beads, even when the sum has been presented many times. The jump from single units to the concept of 10 can also cause confusion, and needs much careful planning, concrete examples and constant revision to ensure this concept is properly learned.

Communication, speech and language skills

Many preschool and infant children present with severe language delay, and thus speech therapy is essential and should be included in the Statement of Need. They can be quite inventive in getting across their meaning, either by the use of 'home-made' signs and gestures, or by more recognised means such as Makaton.

Other options to communicate should also be available to prevent frustration and consequent tantrums. These could include picture boards to facilitate making choices or requests, such as favourite tasks, going to the toilet, mum, dad, staff members etc. Makaton has been successfully used with a number of children and there have been no reports of children relying on sign language once oral speech is sufficiently developed. (See Chapter 2 for a discussion the variations in speech and language problems).

Physical education

Physical activity can be very difficult for most children with PWS, due to their poor muscle tone, although those on growth hormone may find it much easier. Generally speaking, simple movements such as running, skipping, jumping and hopping can all present children with PWS with challenges. There is also a slight additional risk that poor balance, short stature, and lack of coordination can make the child vulnerable to falling if accidentally pushed by more boisterous children, and so extra care and support may be needed. Some may have the additional complications of obesity, scoliosis or weak knee joints. However, it is very important to ensure that some exercise is taken. Exercise can definitely help improve muscle tone and is also instrumental in burning off extra calories. Most young children are keen to try, but need a great deal of motivation and encouragement when they find an activity difficult. Working towards rewards can sometimes work, and plenty of praise is essential.

To help improve balance and jumping skills, use PE mats as 'stepping stones', placing them very close together to begin with, gradually pulling them further apart as ability and confidence grows. The mats can also be used to help with maths skills. Number each mat so that each has to be jumped onto in number order. Again, the number of mats can be increased as number awareness increases.

Large apparatus can present a particular problem, especially if peers are racing ahead, and extra adult help may be required here, with special praise if a particularly difficult piece of apparatus has been attempted.

Obese children will encounter additional difficulties, especially with breathing and stamina, and may need to stop for short rest breaks. If a child of this age is so obese that they find it almost impossible to take part in PE lessons, it may be necessary, with the cooperation of parents, to involve outside agencies such as community health to try to reduce weight, as this could become a life-threatening problem.

Dance and music are often good motivators, especially if children are allowed to choose the music. Aerobic type exercises are very good. Bean bags, throwing and catching, can improve hand—eye coordination as well as improving turn-taking skills. Team games are also important, although extra input may be needed for those who find social skills difficult. Physiotherapy may be required to provide an individual programme for those with particular physical problems.

Children with PWS often excel at swimming and may swim relatively long distances. If swimming lessons are available, full advantage should be taken of them.

Physical exercise can be brought into the ordinary classroom situation. For instance, in order to improve the muscles in the upper body, floor puzzles and games can be used, so that the child has to work from an all fours position, which is helpful in improving trunk, shoulders and hip stability (Lloyd and Deusterhaus-Minor 1995).

Juniors

By the time the child with PWS reaches junior school age, some may already be showing signs of significant intellectual delay, while others will require perhaps just a little extra support to keep up. However, sometimes behavioural problems also begin to develop at this age, and although the child can keep up intellectually with their peers, their behaviours may begin to impede their overall development. Immature emotions and social skills can also prevent the child from using their intellectual skills to the full extent. The obsession with food is also likely to become stronger. Some children, although by no means all, will steal food and money from other children, or beg food from others. In such cases, strong environmental controls need to be in place, including food and money locked away, and closer adult supervision of the child's movements.

If possible or appropriate, 'mixed' teaching may be beneficial, where the child spends part of the day with a mainstream class, perhaps doing project based tasks, and another part of the day working in language or other special needs units to develop basic skills.

Table 4.2 shows the strengths and weaknesses of junior age children, as described by teachers. Again, no one child would have all the strengths and weaknesses indicated here.

Skills patterns can be very erratic. For example, one child could match the word 'green' to a green pencil, but when asked to give a green pencil to the teacher, was unable to do this. Matching groups of identical numbers of objects may present few problems, but identifying the actual number could be (Waters 1991).

The following are some suggestions to improve the performance of children of this age group, which can be applied across curriculum subjects:

Strengths	Weaknesses
Friendly, sociable	Poor social skills with peers/immature
Puzzles	Stubborn, wants own way
Independent	Bossy with other children, argumentative
Good number concept/mental arithmetic	Poor number concept/poor problem solving skills
Good memory for people and events	Poor short term memory
Good sense of humour	Low self-esteem/confidence
Helpful, caring	Tantrums, sometimes severe
Reading and books	Literal interpretation of words
Determined, diligent, persists to finish	Poor motivation to stay on task/complete work in given time
Good concentration	Lack of concentration, easily distracted
Very careful worker/perfectionist	Impatient
Writing skills	Writing skills
Remembering things which are going to happen	Unable to understand complex instructions
Polite	Manipulative/attention-seeking
Interest in general knowledge/world around	Speech disorder
Self reliant/can occupy self	Anxious/confused in new situations. Upset by new routines
Organised	Hoarding
Music/art	Obsessional behaviour
Computer skills	Scissor skills
Good communication skills	Incessant talking/irrelevant talk/inappropriate shouting out/echolaic speech
Home economics	Aggressive and violent behaviour towards self and others
Can be trusted to take messages	Turn-taking, sharing
Willing to learn	PE
Responds well to younger children	Lying

Table 4.2 Strengths and weaknesses of junior school age children, as described by teachers in a questionnaire carried out the PWSA (UK) 1998.

- use of a computer, word processor or similar technological aid, if handwriting is difficult due to low muscle tone or poor pencil control;
- use a keyguard with computers to prevent the child pressing down more than one key at once;
- use visual prompts as well as verbal instructions. Make extensive use of photos, illustrations and videos;
- motivate the child with the promise of a favourite activity if the work is completed (and always keep the promise);
- break complex instructions down into small steps, or make lists and flow charts to aid the progress of logical thought;
- set targets for independence skills (i.e. dressing and personal hygiene);
- provide one to one work or close monitoring of group work;
- provide a structured day, with visual timetable to refer to;
- repeat and rehearse learning in a number of different settings;

- present clearly defined tasks with clear outcomes;
- use a non-confrontational approach;
- praise, reward and challenge;
- present new ideas and most difficult tasks early in the day;
- allow to choose own task once a day/week;
- use competitive small group work (if the child is capable of winning for some of the time);
- use formal teaching;
- provide early warning of changes to the usual routine, and clear explanations;
- present interesting tasks just before break and lunch times to divert attention away from food;
- provide quiet environment with no distractions for work on new or difficult tasks.

Literacy skills

Although reading and writing is often referred to as a strength in children with PWS, they may still have some difficulties in this area. If pencil control or coordination remains a problem, many find word processing much easier. However, handwriting exercises are still helpful for those who are willing to persist at a task. There is sometimes a lack of imagination in writing; often the focus of a story will be food, and it will contains long lists of what was had to eat. Story-telling may not move very far away from the child's own experiences, or will reflect something they saw on the television the previous night.

Reading may involve a lot of one to one work, with well-structured lessons, progressing to the next step only when the previous one has been thoroughly learned. Phonic skills are often lacking, and children may remember words rather than reading them. Speech and language disorders can also impact on reading skills. When reading out loud, 'clapped' syllables may help.

Although reading may be relatively fluent, comprehension may still be poor. This can cause problems, because the child may be keen to move on to the next book, and may resist attempts to record or discuss the content of the current book, saying they have already read it. A firm approach is necessary here, so that the child is clear that the next book will not be attempted until they have answered questions on the first book. They may need one to one support to do this.

Numeracy skills

In mathematics, concrete and spatial tasks are generally better understood, and should be used wherever possible to underpin abstract concepts. For some children, even basic number concept is difficult, and counting can be problematic; there may be very poor memory for number bonds. Constant revision, small steps, and bringing mathematical skills into other areas of life (e.g. counting peas on the plate at lunch!) may be helpful.

Trying to solve maths-based problems, especially those in the form of a written narrative, is usually difficult, particularly in determining which method should be used. One to one help should be available to break the narrative into small steps, together with the provision of concrete examples of how it works.

The difficulties which children with PWS have in adapting to new ideas makes maths particularly difficult for them. They may only be able to use one method at a time, completely forgetting a previous method when a new one is introduced.

Physical education

As children with PWS get older, motivation to join in with PE often gets less. Peers are increasingly more able, additional weight may have been gained, and a history of failure may affect self confidence. However, PE remains a crucial part of the curriculum to help the general health and well-being of children with PWS, and encouragement and patience are vital. Music and dance can be helpful, but often individual physiotherapy input is needed. All the ideas provided in the previous section for infants are also appropriate at this stage.

Child study by Deborah Thackray

John is four years old. He attends part-time at an LEA mainstream nursery school. The nursery is resourced by the LEA for twelve SEN children with additional support of a specialist teacher and nursery nurse. John travels to and from nursery in a taxi with an escort.

So far there are not signficant problems around eating. If other children have sweets to share for birthdays, John is offered an alternative of fruit which he is very happy with. He does have some difficulties with sharing and turn taking. He can become quite distressed about these situations. It is usually resolved by explanation and praise when he responds to the critical request.

John is developing a good visual memory. He can recognise his own name. There is evidence of emergent writing. John enjoys sharing books with an adult and listens attentively at group story-time.

John is able to match and sort by colour, shape, size, type etc. He counts by rote to three. He is aware of numbers in the environment. He is becoming aware of time and often points to the clock or adult's watch when talking about events past, present, future, e.g. time for his taxi/been swimming.

John shows an exceptional ability to concentrate. He will persevere at an activity up to 30 minutes. John is able to use his many experiences in his wonderful creative and imaginative play. John's drawing (see Fig 4.2) was done when John had just completed his sponsored bike ride (10 laps). He came straight into the room and sat the mark-making table. He chose a blue biro and using his left hand made tiny circular movements. He did not lift his pen from the paper. His first pattern made a large oval shape towards the top of the paper. John said 'round and round', then pointing towards the window said 'outside'. He continued filling the paper with same pattern for 20 minutes.

John experiences the most difficulty in the area of speech and language. He is able to form sentences, but his speech can be difficult to understand. He often uses gestures to help aid understanding.

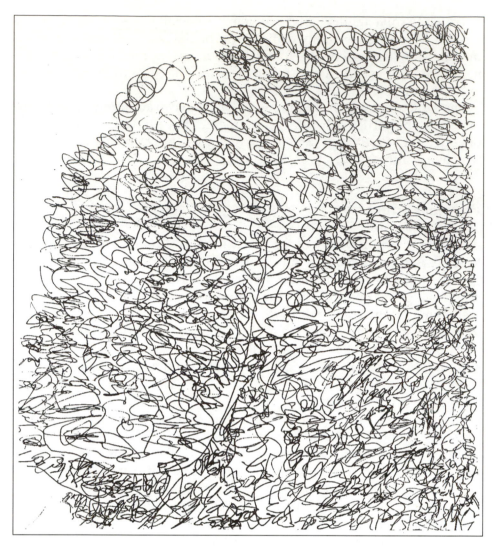

Figure 4.2 John's drawing after his sponsored bike ride.

In order to support John's education, the following are provided:

• planned input based on IEP targets;

Figure 4.3 John drawing a bicycle.

• support within the mainstream activities for the majority of the time, but also time for work in small groups and one to one situations.

John is a very happy and sociable little boy. He has a wonderful sense of humour and is very confident in many situations.

John sat for 15 minutes drawing a bicycle from observation, (see Figure 4.3). He talked about his bike 'at home', about 'Daddy's bike', and about the wheels that were big and went round and round. He drew a large spiral starting from the centre.

Chapter 5

Secondary Age Children: Classroom and Behaviour Management

Figure 5.1 Katie, aged 14. Weight has been well controlled at home and school. Note the immature dress sense and physical characteristics.

The transition from primary to secondary level requires very careful consideration, particularly if the child has been in mainstream school at primary level. As Table 2.1 shows, the child is most likely to change from a mainstream school to a special school at this age. This may not necessarily be because the child cannot cope adequately at an intellectual level. Often behavioural problems or emotional immaturity become more apparent, and allowances need to be made for the fact that youngsters are unable to keep up on a social and emotional level with their peers. This becomes increasingly obvious as other children reach puberty, and the child with PWS may often be very delayed in this area.

Careful consideration and monitoring needs to be given to those who remain, or who are thinking of remaining, within the mainstream structure. This will probably involve classroom assistance for some of the time, depending on the individual, but there are other factors which need to be taken into account:

- Is the level of classroom support adequate to ensure that occasional or frequent temper outbursts, which may increase in the teenage years, are dealt with firmly and with minimal disruption to the rest of the class?
- Is the level of support adequate to ensure that a child who has poor self-control around food will not have easy access to self-service style catering, tuckshops, and other pupils' school bags and lunch boxes?
- Is the journey to and from school 'safe' in terms of possible opportunities for obtaining food from shops and cafes (some older children with PWS may take food from shops without paying for it).

The secondary school child in mainstream

- Is the school spread over several buildings and locations, or does it have a large number of steps and stairs? If so, can the timetable be arranged so that lessons are held in adjoining classrooms, or can allowances be made for a child with PWS arriving late in class, due to the slowness with which many children with PWS habitually move?
- Are other pupils in the school generally aware of the consideration required for peers with special needs?
- Is sex education handled in a sympathetic way, or can it be modified for the needs of the child with PWS (see section on sex education in Chapter 6)?
- Can the school make allowances for a pupil who tires easily, and may fall asleep in the afternoons?

Transferring to a special needs school or unit

The child who transfers to a special needs school from mainstream may also need additional support. They need to understand that they have not 'failed' in mainstream, but that they can do better and their needs will be better met within the special needs system. Probably the best way of ensuring this transition takes place smoothly is for the child to attend their new school for one day a week in the term preceding the move.

Dietary needs and supervision

The need to keep to a lower calorie diet can become even more difficult at the secondary school stage, particularly in mainstream, where the general environment of tuck shops, snacks on the way to school, open-plan and self-service dining rooms, other pupils keeping sweets and crisps in bags and pockets, can all spell great temptation to the pupil with PWS. They may also begin to resent having to have meals controlled, when their peers are free to make choices. It may be helpful for a staff member or assistant to sit with the pupil at lunch and help them to make healthy eating choices – especially if that assistant also needs to lose weight. Alternatively, if there are other pupils in the school who have to have special diets, there could be a special diet table or serving hatch for such pupils.

The task is easier where there is close cooperation between home and school, but sometimes the parents may feel that they do not wish their son or daughter to be prevented from eating. This can prove difficult, particularly if the pupil's eating habits or weight are causing great concern, and it may be necessary to involve outside agencies such as community health or the PWSA (UK) to find a solution to this problem. Wherever possible, the pupil with PWS should be involved in the decision making process.

In some cases, greater environmental controls may need to be in place. These may include:

- keeping food waste bins in a secure area;
- ensuring that the pupil with PWS stays for as short a time as possible in the dining area (i.e. that they are not left sitting surrounded by leftovers);
- in extreme cases, there may be a need to warn other pupils;
- one to one support at break and lunch times;
- warning ancillary staff not to give food to the youngster with PWS.

Skin-picking or spot-picking

Skin-picking seems to worsen or first become evident during adolescence. Locations for skin-picking vary widely, the most common being the hands, arms, feet, face and head, but more secretive behaviours occur at night or in the toilet where other areas of the body (including sometimes the rectum) are the targets. Variations on this type of behaviour also occur, e.g.: picking 'fluff' off clothing, pulling out hair, pulling other people's hair or clothing, and using pins and other objects to make a wound.

It is thought that skin-picking behaviour is actually a pleasurable activity for people with PWS, as it releases endorphins in the brain. Their high pain threshold means that painful sensations are unlikely to stop them. Skin-picking often becomes worse if the child is anxious, confused, tired or too hot. There is no guaranteed way of preventing this behaviour, but some suggestions are:

- gently draw the youngster's attention to what they are doing, and provide something else for them to do with their hands;
- provide plasters and ointment for the youngster to cover and treat the wound themselves;
- initiate a more physical activity;
- provide a 'star chart', and reward if picking does not occur and a long-standing wound is healed;
- cool the room down, or place the child in a cooler spot;
- if skin-picking behaviour is getting worse, try to identify if there is an external source of anxiety.

Physical needs

The youngster with PWS is likely to be considerably shorter than their peers, especially if they have not been entered on a growth hormone programme. Classroom furniture may need adaptations to ensure that the youngster's feet can touch the floor when sitting – this is easier for balance and less fatiguing. Similarly, stabilised steps may be needed for work tables and benches to allow ease of working.

Organisational skills

These can vary from child to child, but there do seem to be children with PWS at both ends of this spectrum. On the one hand there is the youngster who is obsessively tidy and extremely possessive. Rulers and pens have to be laid out in a particular manner, or clothes put on in a certain order, with outbursts and stubbornnesss occurring if they are thwarted in these actions. These youngsters may be helped by offering more choices and by role play.

On the other hand, some youngsters have very poor organisational skills. They may carry several bags around with them, rooting through them all to find a pen, and leaving one or more things behind in a classroom. Often if an item is lost, other people will be blamed without any proof whatsoever, or a temper outburst may occur. Such youngsters need very clear instructions, and perhaps support to choose which items to take to a lesson, leaving the remainder in a locker or other secure place. Simple steps to finding lost items could be written down for the person to refer to, possibly in the form of a flow chart, e.g.:

- Check your bag again carefully – take each item out in turn and shake any books.
- Where did you last have the item?

- When was the last time you can remember using it?
- Look in these places.
- If you still can't find it, report it to your teacher or your classroom assistant. Has anyone else seen it?
- If you still can't find it, report it to lost property.
- Ask the teacher or classroom assistant for a replacement you can borrow.
- Don't get upset – remember that most of the things you've lost, you always find again.
- Don't blame others.

Emotional outbursts and stubborn behaviour

The techniques outlined in Chapter 3 are still appropriate at this age, but in a few cases the outbursts may become abusive, aggressive or violent. This should not be tolerated, and there may be a case for withdrawal of privileges, or the threat of withdrawal. However, it should be remembered that an outburst may have been triggered by an outside event in the person's life, and efforts should be made to find out if this is the case. If the behaviour becomes unmanageable, then professional outside help should be sought from a psychiatrist, or a possible transfer to a more suitable school should be considered.

Sometimes the pupil can be humoured out of stubborn behaviour. Another strategy is to ignore them until they move on to the next task. One proposal was to take a photograph of the person when they are having an outburst, which can be used as a reminder to them of how other people are seeing them when this happens (Waters 1991).

Social skills

The gap in emotional and social skills between youngsters with PWS and their peers becomes increasingly evident at the secondary level, and this is often one of the major reasons why integration into mainstream may not be successful. The youngster with PWS may be still relating to others at the level of a much younger child. If they are bullied or teased, they will break into uncontrollable tears or become physically aggressive. They may see nothing wrong with hugging and cuddling members of staff.

Apart from the autistic theory, one of the most probable causes of lack of social skills is the delay in emotional development, which may be due to hypothalamic dysfunction. Some children with PWS are functioning at an emotional level as young as that of a three year old child, even though their intellectual age may be much higher. It would seem that some children with PWS want to join in, but do not know how to do this (see Figure 5.2). They should be encouraged to join in group games and discussions wherever possible, as well as attending social skills sessions if these are available.

Another factor is that unfortunately some children with PWS may have developed unpleasant habits of lying, stealing and aggressiveness which other children do not like. The other children may also, consciously or not, exclude the child with PWS from their activities because of perceived 'differences'. A general rule of zero tolerance of bullying, teasing, lying, stealing and aggressiveness may help with both sides of this problem.

Figure 5.2 Youngsters with PWS often 'circle around' groups of other children.

Unawareness of personal space can also be problematic. The youngster with PWS may stand very close to the person they are speaking to. A gentle reminder to 'step backward' may all be that is required here. Praise the person when they are standing at a correct distance without being reminded.

Encouragement to join lunch time and after hours clubs can be helpful, especially if the person is made to feel wanted when they get there, and can make an acknowledged useful contribution. Many youngsters with PWS feel safer and less anxious in the structured environment of an adult-led club than having to fend for themselves within a group of their peers.

The person with PWS can be helped with social skills, provided the timetable and the statement can accommodate it. One determined parent managed to get the needs for social skills training written into his daughter's Statement of Needs. He writes:

By the beginning of Year 8 in secondary school, Catherine was desperately lonely, with no friends near her own age. When she talked about 'just walking around' during the lunch break, because it felt less lonely than staying in one place, it was difficult to be sure who was nearest to tears – her or me . . .

Whilst the need for social skills training was included in the statement, nothing was done until the beginning of the fifth term at secondary school when a small group comprising Catherine and a few other children with similar needs started to meet with a teacher one lunch time each week. Her father continues:

Initially, they just played board games and got to know one another. Then the teacher gradually introduced discussion of how people relate to one another and explained concepts such as personal space, eye contact, listening, turn-taking etc.; soon this led on to role playing, with feedback and discussion.

Within a term Catherine's life was transformed and she became much happier and more positive at school. She no longer dreaded breaks and lunchtimes because of loneliness. Initially, the children involved formed a friendship group and for some of them, certainly for Catherine, it was a welcome new experience to have someone to meet with and hang out with during breaks. Of course, given the nature of the children involved, this ideal did not last: Catherine and two girls formed a threesome, but then one of the girls became very threatened by Catherine being a friend of her friend and it became a little unpleasant. Catherine discussed the situation with her teacher before telling me how she was going to deal with it; it was then that I realized what remarkable progress she had made: 'Dad, I'm going to give them some space,' and she clearly understood the concept and its purpose (Williams 1996).

Several ideas to help with social skills training are discussed by Whitman and Greenswag (1995). These include:

- The timing game. In this game, situations are printed in large letters on cards that can be read aloud in turn (e.g. teacher is talking to a visitor to the class, teacher is working with another pupil, teacher is walking round the classroom). Each person in the group has a response card to indicate whether the situation read out by the leader is a good time to start a conversation. The group can then discuss responses.
- The open/closed questions game. Questions are printed in large letters and read aloud. Each person in the group has a response card to say whether the question requires a one or two word answer or a lengthier one, stimulating conversation.
- The assertive game. Descriptions of assertive, aggressive, and non-assertive behaviours are written or read out, and group members must try to decide which is which.

Obsessional behaviours and perseveration

All the strategies described in chapters 3 and 7 to deal with obsessional behaviours and perseveration can also be used with this age group, but it is at this age that perseverative behaviour and speech can become particularly problematic, as it prevents the child – and sometimes the rest of the class and the teacher – from moving on to the next task.

Perseverative behaviour and speech occurs when the youngster continually reverts to a topic (often food based, but not always), or asks the same question over and over again. There is still a debate going on among researchers as to whether this is a behavioural problem or a linguistic one, i.e. has the child just not understood the answer, or been unable to process the instructions, or are they physically stuck on that particular word, phrase or idea? One expert in the USA contends that perseveration behaviour is not an obsession, but rather 'a function of a nervous system whose on/off switch often gets stuck in the 'on' positition.' (Whitman 1993) Whatever the reasons – and they may be different for different youngsters – some strategies are offered below to help with this behaviour:

- Do not continue to argue, explain or reason with the child – they are unlikely to internalise what you are saying, and will become increasingly confused and distressed.

- Divert the youngster's attention away from the topic by suggesting that something else is talked about.
- If the child is asking the same question over and over, ask them to repeat back the answer. If they do this correctly, reassure them that they have it right.
- If 'I don't know' is the answer because it genuinely is not known, an explanation may be needed to tell them why the answer isn't known and when it might be. Otherwise they may think that if they keep asking, sooner or later someone will know, or simply that they are just being fobbed off or ignored.
- Put time limits on topics. Say 'we will talk about this for x more minutes', set an alarm, or show the hands on the clock and then firmly close the subject.
- Sometimes the repetition may be because the youngster is unsure or anxious about something. Break the explanation down into very small steps to ensure that everything is well understood.
- Be aware that if someone replies to the question every time it is asked, this may constitute a 'reward' to the child, and they will continue to perseverate because they know they will get a response.

Hoarding

Whilst many youngsters like to build collections some children with PWS, go far beyond this. Clear rules and limits need to be enforced for the whole class if hoarding is presenting a problem (e.g. only one pencil case per person). Alternatively, youngsters can be encouraged to donated excess articles to the school fair or to charity. However, teachers should be aware that hoarding behaviour which is stopped may be replaced by another activity such as constantly writing lists or menus.

Difficulty in adapting to changes in routine

This, like many other PWS behaviours, may have been over-tolerated in younger children, as 'something he will grow out of'. Unfortunately this is rarely the case, because of the emotional immaturity of many youngsters. In the secondary school environment there is less likelihood of tolerance, especially if the reaction to a change is an emotional outburst or a stubborn refusal to move. There are many different strategies which can be tried, but it is unlikely they will all work all of the time. Here are the most commonly used:

- always try to advise the whole class in advance – don't 'surprise' them;
- warn the pupil with PWS first, before the rest of the class is told;
- if possible, warn parents as well so that the matter can be discussed at home;
- give known alternative well in advance e.g. 'if the weather is wet, we will . . .';
- if a change is totally unforeseen, warn class to get ready for a 'big surprise', and if possible ensure that a classroom assistant is on hand to sit with the pupil with PWS;
- use techniques mentioned earlier to prevent perseveration on the topic.

Other suggestions are also given in Chapter 3 for children of a developmentally younger age.

Tiredness

Whilst tiredness can be an issue at an earlier age, it can become a far greater problem at the secondary school stage. Because the pressures are possibly greater, as well as many pupils becoming obese, youngsters with PWS may be even more prone to tiredness than they were when they were younger. It can be offset to some degree by employing the following strategies:

- ensure that the room is not too hot or too cold;
- open windows (as long as this does not allow distracting noise from outside to interfere with concentration);
- try to keep lessons practice-based in the afternoons, rather than lecture style;
- liaise with parents over sleeping patterns at home – does the pupil have disturbed sleeping patterns at night, and would a check for sleep apnoea (see Chapter 1) be advisable?

It may be necessary, however, to acknowledge that a half-hour sleep can be beneficial to the pupil, who will be less likely to be fretful and irritable if this is allowed.

Self-management of behaviour

Various techniques can be tried to help the youngster with PWS manage their own behaviour. These could include:

- simple anger management techniques such as counting to ten or breathing deeply;
- self-talk – teaching the child to hold a conversation with themselves about what they should be doing, or to remind themselves of what happened last time the same situation occurred;
- role plays;
- negotiating contracts for good behaviour with teachers and assistants;
- discussion and self-recognition of where improvements are needed.

There is perhaps an onus on the rest of the class to make allowances, and teachers should consider whether a class discussion is appropriate to give them some insight into what it is like to have PWS. One boy with PWS who was in mainstream school decided on his own initiative to tell the class about his problems. He borrowed a video from the PWSA (UK) and gave a short talk, and found that his classmates were far more tolerant after that.

It is very important that a youngster with PWS is included within the management programme. A good example of this is described by Lesley Almond in Goodger *et al.* (1996), when describing her experience with a young teenage boy who came to the residential school where she works:

When pupil X arrived . . . I assessed his physical, social and emotional needs and planned a relevant programme to include a low calorie diet, suitable physical activities and a structured routine in order to support his development through adolescence. A highly professional job was done by all – or so I thought.

Unfortunately I had failed to take into consideration the narrow and somewhat rigid perception that the child with PWS has. He did not agree with my assessment and planning of his care. He did not feel 'in control' of what was happening, and control was very important to him.

Because pupil X's expressive abilities exceeded his comprehension, he liked to 'save face' and to be always seen as knowledgeable, articulate and 'in control'. Perhaps control is more important to him that to others, because of his lack of control in other areas of his life e.g. eating and temperamental outbursts. By imposing a programme of care on him, I had taken control out of his hands and retained that all-important power for myself. We had reached an impasse.

It became clear through working with pupil X, that one of us would have to alter our perception of the situation, if we were to progress. Because of the syndrome he has a rigid, narrow and stubborn outlook, particularly when working with new people. I was the professional, therefore I was the one who had to change.

Goodger goes on to relate how the programme was re-planned in agreement with pupil X, emphasising that a good relationship of trust and affection needed to be in place before her pupil felt secure enough to finally admit that he did not know everything and was not always right. Even then, constant liaison with home and other staff was necessary during the first term, to fine-tune every aspect of his care and education – just one minor thing going wrong was enough to upset the youngster and potentially eradicate all the progress that had been made so far.

School outings

School outings and trips can present a host of difficulties if not carefully planned in advance. Lynn Langlands in Goodger *et al.* (1996) describes a simple study trip to a nearby town and the consequent need for support for her pupil. This included:

- supervision to prevent him stealing tempting objects and food;
- the choice of the right peer partner for him;
- decisions on how food would be presented – packed lunches being best. Being aware that the pupil might not be able to concentrate on his work until after lunch;
- seating in the coach – as youngsters with PWS tend to fall asleep they need to be in a secure seat that they will not fall out of;
- thinking ahead about unforseen events that could provoke an outburst, making provision in advance for a member of staff to follow the pupil to ensure he came to no harm.

Child study by Toby Salt

Anna is 16 years old and is in Year 11 at an LEA maintained day/residential special school for pupils with 'moderate learning difficulties'. Anna is a weekly boarder at this school which has 117 pupils on roll aged 7–16 years. Educationally Anna achieves at an average to above average level, for a pupil at this school. At her last annual review, the following was reported:

National Curriculum Level 2 in English, Level 3 in Maths, and Level 2 in Science. Reading age (Daniels and Diack) 8.6 years.

Psychological advice reports 'poor articulation', and that her 'understanding is of a slightly higher level than her performance in academic skills'.

Anna does have particular behavioural difficulties. These include: difficulties in relating to peers and adults, obsessive conversations/repetition, a liking of routines and fixation on certain times (e.g. meal times!), 'tantrums' if she feels she is being unfairly treated or challenged, stubbornness, and stealing other children's sweets or snacks. When Anna does have a 'tantrum', she will become rigid, affix herself to an immovable object and refuse to communicate or move. In such a situation it is nearly impossible to talk her around and she will obstinately stay for as long as an hour. Anna reacts best if initially you agree with her complaint and do not get into an argument with her. Sometimes the teacher will consciously wait until a few minutes before meal time – knowing she is more likely to cooperate! Her parents have been telephoned and asked to speak to her, and on rare occasions staff have had to physically remove her, if she is putting herself at risk.

The stealing is rare but is difficult to deal with as she frequently denies the offence, despite obvious evidence. We rely on parents' support to get Anna to use some of her pocket money to replace stolen items.

It is likely that Anna will require a specialist post-16 college placement. The school has educated Anna on healthy eating and she is offered a special diet for breakfasts and evening meals. A plentiful supply of fruit is offered for snacks. At parties, Anna needs sensitive supervision and support to help her not to eat to the point of sickness. Anna is a kind girl, who is liked by many staff, but she requires considerable support and consistency, and can test staff patience and teamwork to the limit.

Chapter 6

Secondary Age Children: Educational Techniques

Figure 6.1 Laura is in mainstream school with 25 hour support.

The range of abilities precludes any specific suggestions for educational techniques for secondary age pupils. They are likely to range from pupils who have the bare minimum of literacy and numeracy skills to those who do not fall within the learning disabilities range.

While the majority of children with PWS are unlikely to progress as far as GCSE level, there are some who can, and do, sit these examinations. Three success stories recently reported to the PWSA (UK) were:

- a boy who obtained grade Es in English and German, and Fs in Home Economics and Maths.
- a girl who obtained a grade D for Art, Es for English and Drama, F for Science and G for Maths.
- a boy who obtained Es for Art and Design.

Figure 6.1 is a photo of Laura who has PWS and is successful in the mainstream setting, with support.

Table 6.1. shows the strengths and weaknesses of secondary school age pupils, as described by teachers. As with previous age groups, areas which are strengths in some pupils can appear as weaknesses in others, and no one person is likely to have all the strengths all the weaknesses.

Many of the educational techniques used at primary school level can still be utilised for secondary school pupils, especially those with severe or moderate learning difficulties. However, some additional methods which may help within the secondary school setting are as follows:

- use of computer/word processor for those with handwriting difficulties;
- use of educational computer games to aid learning, especially where visual reinforcement is needed;
- use of individual research and project work, especially for homework tasks;

General abilities and methods of working to obtain best results

Strengths	Weaknesses
Happy, kind	Temper tantrums
Sense of humour	Impatience
Friendly, sociable	Little understanding of others' feelings
Reading	Domineering, wanting to be first
Art, drawing	Poor concentration
Acting ability	Interferes in other pupils' work
Music	Echolaic speech
Likes responsibility	Comprehension
Determination, persistence	Mathematics
Sense of fairness	Science
Willing to join in	Abusive to staff
Computers, IT	Stubborn
Keen to please	Immature
Individual project work	PE/Gross motor problems
Food technology/home economics	Large group discussions
Good general knowledge	Problem solving skills
Easily interested in new topics	Perseverative speech
Simple construction technology	Aggressive and violent towards self and/or others
Good relationship with adults	Vulnerable to abuse by others/easily led
Attention to detail	Limited imagination
Neat appearance	Speech problems
Good memory	Dislike of change to routine/resistant to new ideas
Horticulture	Unable to deal with teasing

Table 6.1 Strengths and weaknesses of secondary age pupils with PWS, as described by teachers in a questionnaire carried out by the PWSA (UK) 1998.

- giving individual attention where necessary to motivate and move on to next step;
- praise and challenge;
- keeping maths and science tasks as concrete as possible.

Be aware that, like their younger counterparts, pupils of this age do tire easily, and quite often even more quickly than younger children, because of weight gain and additional work pressures. Allowances should be made for this, possibly by allowing time for a nap or presenting more difficult tasks in the morning.

Auditory processing may still prove problematic, so that verbal instructions should be backed up with written or pictorial ones, or asking the individual to repeat what has been said to them. Small step instructions are invariably best.

Timed assignments and exams can be particularly difficult for several reasons:

- the pupil may fixate on trying to get one part of the task done perfectly;
- they may have little sense of how fast time is passing;
- they may experience increased anxiety through perceived outside pressure;
- they may be easily distracted.

Suggestions for helping with these are:

- plenty of practice beforehand and encouragement to just get as much down as possible;
- the use of a combination of a watch/clock and a visual display to say how far through the exercise or exam they should be by a certain time, with instructions to move on if they have not finished;
- the use of word-processors, or human helpers in exams;
- teaching relaxation techniques, e.g. deep breathing;
- placing the youngster near the front of the class, and away from windows.

English/literacy skills

While it is generally the case that people with PWS have better literacy than numeracy skills, English can still be difficult for those with PWS, with reading ages varying between two to six years below chronological age. Reading may be fluent, but comprehension may be lacking, requiring extra support to ensure that what is read has been correctly understood. Additionally, errors can be made in reading and comprehension because of a disregard of punctuation. Sometimes too-literal interpretations will be made of the text. Many will continue to find handwriting difficult, and may produce better work using a word processor. Handwriting may be too small or too large, with an extremely erratic use of punctuation.

Sometimes the obsessive need to check and re-check work hinders progress. One suggestion to help the youngster is to ask them to just write down every thought as it comes into their head, with the rule of 'no rubbing out', then, later, to go through it with the teacher or classroom assistant looking for errors and writing it correctly.

Weekly graded spelling lists drawn from classwork can provide valuable revision of work and vocabulary extension. Reading books should reflect the youngster's own interests, but there should also be the opportunity to read imaginative works with figurative language. Support will be needed to work on the latter, as the youngster will probably find it difficult to understand unless someone is working closely with them to explain non-factual concepts and metaphors.

Essay writing may consist of long 'lists' of food or other items which the person is obsessive about. Some youngsters seem to particularly enjoy soaps on television, and also police-based stories and murder mysteries. Work could reflect these interests, e.g. discussing an episode of a soap shown the previous night, or asking youngsters to suggest what might happen next to the characters.

Many youngsters show a great ability with Wordsearch type puzzles. This may reflect the ability to concentrate and focus on detail. Two teenage girls with PWS known to the author spent a car journey lasting three hours competing with one another to complete Wordsearches first, accompanied by much hilarity. These can be used to improve vocabulary and spelling, and can be extended to ask the pupil to use each word they find in the Wordsearch in a sentence they have constructed themselves.

Mathematics/ numeracy skills

This can often present the greatest area of difficulty, although this is by no means the rule. Some youngsters with PWS may still have problems counting to 10 by secondary school age, while others are able to cope with most types of calculations as well as graphs etc. Life skills such as shopping can be used to help with time and money, as can number games, simple puzzles and using concrete objects to aid understanding. Geometry-based work can also prove difficult. 3D spatial awareness may be limited; tracing over shapes may help. Methods learned one day may be forgotten by the next, so that repetitive work is essential. Quizzes, small steps and practical work are usually the best methods of working.

The difference between fractions, decimals and whole numbers may be a particularly difficult concept for the more able pupil with PWS to grasp. All problems should be kept as concrete as possible to aid understanding in this area.

Other areas of the curriculum

Because of the basic difficulties that exist in numeracy and literacy, other areas of the curriculum are likely to prove equally problematic. Humanities, especially if project-based, can produce good work, but those who have poor literacy skills will struggle to keep up.

In science, there may be a basic lack of understanding of why something is being done, and difficulty in reporting back experiments and drawing conclusions from them. Experiments may need to be repeated more than once, so that the youngster can begin to understand the nature of cause and effect.

Difficulties can also be experienced in understanding. For instance, although a word like 'volume' may be used to indicate a quantity of liquid, to the youngster it may only mean 'sound' – especially as they will be familiar with it from TV and radio controls. As has been shown, rigid thinking can provoke anxiety and confusion, so try to foresee where this kind of problem may arise, and work with the pupil on the meanings in advance.

Specific safety risks may arise around the following areas:

- Clumsiness arising from dyspraxia, lack of coordination and balance, and lack of spatial awareness can create problems when working on experiments or with cooking, metalwork or woodwork tools – close supervision may be required.
- A propensity to put liquids and food into the mouth, or to lick the fingers after handling liquids may mean that close supervision and visual warnings are appropriate.
- Physical lack of awareness of heat and cold when cooking or working on experiments can result in relatively severe burns, which because of their high pain threshold, the person may not be aware of.
- Fascination with fire in some individuals can be a hazard.

Figure 6.2 shows a boy with PWS who functions at six or seven years below his chronological age.

Figure 6.2 A boy with PWS, aged 15, who functions at 8 to 9 year old level

Personal development/ sex education

Sex education needs very careful handling if there is a pupil with PWS in the class, and liaison with home beforehand is recommended. It is unlikely the youngster will be maturing as fast as their peers, and there is every chance that the normal process of sexual development will be delayed or arrested in both boys and girls with Prader-Willi syndrome (see Chapter 1 for further details). However, they do need to have a basic knowledge of sexual relationships, both in terms of knowing what normally happens, and also to protect themselves from sexually-transmitted diseases and abuse. It would be unfair for the teacher to make any particular reference to the pupil with PWS, but it may be wise to include within the lesson references to the fact that not all people develop in the same way, and that not all people can have children.

The PWSA (UK) have produced an information pack for children aged 10 and over, with a separate section for over 14s, which explains PWS in simple language and addresses some of the problems of sexuality (Waters 1999). This may prove a useful teaching aid.

Cookery, home economics, food technology

Opinion tends to be split as to whether it is a good thing for youngsters with PWS to learn to cook or not. There is no doubt that they find this a very pleasurable activity, and many make very good cooks. Much depends on the self-control of the individual and the level of support they have during the cookery lesson. The temptation to eat food or put raw food into the mouth can be lessened by heavy emphasis on food hygiene, but it will not solve the problem entirely. Home–school liaison is particularly important. Some youngsters are allowed to cook as long as the entire product is taken home for consumption and shared amongst all the family, with the individual with PWS getting a share, and plenty of praise. Wherever possible, healthy eating options should be cooked in preference to cakes and biscuits.

Physical education

For youngsters in this age group, physical education can often prove very problematic. If their muscles have not been worked on at an earlier age, they will continue to have great difficulties with all types of movement and coordination, and this may be exacerbated by increasing weight. Added to this is the fact that peers are approaching or going through puberty, whilst the physical development of the youngster with PWS may be very slow or completely lacking. The chances that the child will be subject to bullying and teasing in the changing room about their physical characteristics should not be underestimated. Improving self image for this age group is very important, and every opportunity should be taken to motivate the youngster to join in with PE, praising them when they perform well.

Gentle aerobic exercises are particularly useful, especially if these can be done to music. Take plenty of short breaks of about one to two minutes, but do not allow longer breaks as it becomes more difficult to get started again. One to one throwing and catching exercises, as well as dancing, can help coordination and social skills, especially if a sympathetic peer is chosen as the partner. Balancing exercises are beneficial, but need to start off at a very easy level – e.g. walking along a straight line on the ground. Walking, rambling, horse-riding and exercise bikes can also be favourite activities, provided staffing and resources can allow for these.

One area of PE where many youngsters with PWS can excel is swimming, and many have won medals and certificates for this sport. Besides being a good all-round exercise, it can also help with breathing. Youngsters who are embarrassed to enter the pool because of their physical size could possibly be allowed to change near to the pool entrance and get into the pool before everyone else, leaving when everyone else has left. This does, however, have time or staffing implications, as the youngster is likely to take a long time changing, and may need additional personal support.

The Transition Plan

Youngsters aged 13 or over who have a Statement of Need will be provided with a Transition Plan to set out the arrangements for their education between the ages of 14-19 years, and for their transition to adult services. It is important that as many relevant professionals as possible attend the review meeting, particularly any dietitian, speech therapist or occupational or physiotherapist who works with the child. Educational psychology input will also be very helpful, as well as that of any social workers who are involved with the child and their family.

The youngster will need particular preparation if they are taking part in the review. It can be a very anxious and confusing time for them to be talking about 'when you leave school' and some may see the event as more imminent than it actually is. Equally, unrealistic expectations of what may happen should be carefully discussed. Some youngsters may express the wish to become, for example, vets or doctors, and it is unfair to let them continue to think that this will be possible. They can be gently steered into thinking of other areas of the same field e.g. work as animal rescue shelter helpers or first aiders.

If the youngster is thinking of going on to college, consideration needs to be given as to whether a local college can manage the person's dietary needs, especially if they have severe food-stealing behaviours. Would a residential college be more appropriate? Some very creative thinking may be required to ensure that the youngster is able to move into existing adult services with the minimum of disruption.

Liam's date of birth is 1 May 1987. He attends a special school for children with physical disability. His test scores in October 1998 (aged 11) were:

Spar Word Recognition 7 years 8 months
Spar Spelling   8 years
Young Group Maths   6 years 2 months

Child study by Elizabeth Musson

He has moderate learning difficulties and delayed speech and language development. He needs to wear glasses and his vision is kept under review. His behavioural difficulties impede his educational and social development. When he is in a good mood he is willing and cooperative but he can sulk, cry or shout, refuse to work and be disruptive. He dislikes being wrong and will often question the markings for his work. He is taught in a group of ten and he needs lots of individual attention and reassurance. He is working at Level 2 of the Northern Ireland Curriculum. His word recognition skills are better than his comprehension. He needs one to one attention for work involving comprehension, language and reading development.

In maths he is also working at Level 2 in number but has difficulty with problem solving and logical thinking.

Liam is very good at remembering timetables and when pupils should go for therapy. He likes a structured day and has difficulty coping with change. He is warned if there is to be a change of plan. Fire-drill is particularly difficult – 'Why do we have to leave if there is no fire?'

Liam is very food-orientated. He will tell the teacher when it is break or lunch-time. Most days it is hard to get him out of the classroom on to his bus, but on Wednesday when he goes to Scouts and has a sandwich before Scouts begin, he is first out of the room. The school has to ensure that if there is a new driver on the bus, he knows Liam's diet restrictions.

Liam is usually a pleasant and affectionate child, but in a flash he can change to anger and aggression, and everyone is wrong but him.

Chapter 7

Further Education: Classroom and Behaviour Management

Figure 7.1 Katie, whose photo appeared in Chapter 5, here four years older.

The needs of some students at this stage are so specialised that they cannot easily be catered for within local FE facilities, even those with specialist units for students with learning difficulties. In particular, it may be hard to find the correct placement for students with severe challenging behaviour and/or severe weight or food related problems. Figure 7.1 is a photo of Katie, already seen in Figure 5.1 at age fourteen. Here she is eighteen and has spent the two previous years at a local FE college with greater levels of independence and no supervision over eating

It is important that every effort is made to get a realistic assessment of the student before they enter college. A student who is given a place and then asked to leave six months later because the college cannot cope with their dietary or behavioural problems may feel very rejected. It can take months to overcome this and to find suitable alternatives, during which period the individual and their parents or carers can become very stressed and depressed, with a resultant escalation of weight and behaviour problems. In one case reported by a parent, which it is hoped is very isolated, the student was sent home after only two days and asked not to return, ostensibly because 'she could not find her way around the college'.

On the other hand, a good placement can improve the student's self-esteem, especially if they can obtain certificates for the work they have done, and can help them learn to mix with others of the same age, as well as learning new skills which will help them in the future.

Specific issues around cookery and independent living skills are examined in the next chapter, but dietary supervision generally is a very important factor in the FE environment. Most colleges have open refectories, and students are usually encouraged to make use of the facilities there. Unfortunately for students with PWS, this can be an

Dietary needs and supervision

extremely problematic area. Even if food is plated and served specifically to order, there is still the opportunity to access leftovers from other students' plates, or to sneak food from the displays whilst waiting in the queue. Additional supervision may need to be in place during break and lunch times, and even in free periods. Other risk areas are coin-operated sweets and drinks machines, as well as people leaving money and belongings around which can prove too much of a temptation for a few students with PWS. Other students may need to be warned not to give food to the person with PWS, especially if weight is increasing rapidly.

The importance of positive motivation to support the person with PWS to maintain exisiting weight levels, or even lose weight, should not be underestimated. In one case, a 17 year old girl was placed on a high protein diet which enabled her to lose over 20 pounds in weight over a three month period. However, when the same regime was tried the following year, following signficant weight gain, it was unsuccessful. The main difference between the two situations was that in the first year the girl was in a special education class where the teacher showed daily interest and reinforced the girl's successes on the weight control programme. In the second year the student was integrated into other classes without reinforcement from any teachers (James 1985).

Transport

Transport to and from college can also be an issue, and depends to some extent both on the ability of the student with PWS, and the type of journey that is required. In fact, some students will not have the necessary skills to travel by bus, although this can be worked on, as long as all risks are assessed. A single bus journey which takes the student from home straight to college may be possible, but one involving changes or even waiting outside a newsagent's or petrol station may prove too tempting in terms of food access. There is also the issue of vulnerability to strangers – the offer of a drink or a meal at a cafe from a complete stranger will be one that some students could not refuse.

Helping the student to manage PWS

Some people with PWS are not diagnosed until they reach their late teens or even later. It may be very difficult for them to come to terms with the diagnosis, especially those who previously did not think there was anything particularly 'wrong' with them. It can thus be a particularly traumatic time for all concerned, and some personal counselling may be called for. The PWSA (UK) have produced a free information pack for people with PWS to work through, with a tutor if necessary, which tells them in simple language, and with the aid of puzzles and cartoons, all about PWS, including the medical, dietary and behavioural aspects (Waters 1999).

Home–college liaison

Many colleges expect students to relay messages between home and college themselves, and most students with PWS would be capable of this. Unfortunately, in a few instances, messages may be relayed at one end which were never transmitted from the other: e.g. 'We are going on an outing at college tomorrow. I need £5' (no outing had been planned and the £5 was spent on food), or: 'Mum says she hasn't time to make my sandwiches today and I can buy food from the refectory' (the student used money taken from the parent's purse without her knowledge while the sandwiches had been consumed on the way to college).

It must be emphasised that not all students will do this, but those who can and do should be identified early on, and a policy put in place and understood by all staff and parents or carers that only written, authorised, messages should be acted upon.

Other considerations for supervision

Some students with PWS are prone to wander, or to take a long time to reach the classroom. Visits to the toilet may require some form of supervision if the student begins to spend a long time there. This may be due simply to trying to get out of lessons, but it also increases the opportunities for skin-picking to occur, and even rectal picking has been found to be relatively common (Bhargava *et al.* 1996). There is also the chance that the student may be using the privacy of the toilet to consume stolen or forbidden food items.

Others may leave the campus altogether, either to steal or buy food from shops, or to associate with people who will probably be taking advantage of them. Extra supervision may need to be in place to prevent this.

Social skills

Everything that has been said in previous chapters with regard to relationships with others still applies. This is generally a difficult area for people with PWS and they need a lot of input and support, as well as individual counselling. Group discussions are often very useful for this age group, as long as the subject matter is not a known trigger for a temper outburst. Outings and trips away are also very useful times to help the student with PWS begin to generate meaningful relationships. They could also be encouraged to join lunch-time clubs and drama groups.

Personal relationships and sexual issues

Like everyone else, people with PWS vary in their desire to have personal relationships, although anecdotally it seems that the majority have little interest in sexual relationships. Having said that, there remains a minority of people who seem to have serious challenging behaviour around sexual issues. No studies have been done to confirm this view, which is based on information received from professionals who have contacted the PWSA (UK). These behaviours include inappropriate advances towards other students and staff, masturbation in public, sending sexually explicit letters and notes, and allegations of sexual abuse by others.

The latter is a particularly difficult issue and needs careful investigation. People with PWS are undoubtedly vulnerable to sexual abuse, and may be offered food, money or threats to make them cooperate. Thus all allegations should be taken seriously – several cases of proven serious abuse have already come to light. However, they should not necessarily be taken at face value. Every effort should be made to substantiate allegations. Some people with PWS are extremely good at lying; they can be manipulative, attention-seeking and even vengeful if they think they have been slighted. One case is known to the author where a woman used graphic detail to describe what had been done to her, (presumably gleaned from magazines and television programmes) but staff were able to prove without a shadow of doubt that her alleged abuser was innocent.

Obsessive relationships

Another difficult behaviour is obsession with another person, often a member of staff. The person with PWS wants to know what that person is doing, what they are saying, and will not cooperate with anyone else. One suggestion to manage this is to use a contract system with the person with PWS to change this behaviour. The contract should state that the person spends a specified amount of time (say five to ten minutes) each morning with the favourite staff member. During this time they can review the day's timetable and catch up on each other's news. The person then spends the next hour or so on normal activities. If these are carried out satisfactorily, then part of break time can be spent with the favoured person, and so on throughout the day. As the person becomes more comfortable without the favoured person, the times together can be decreased, although they may not cease completely.

Other behavioural problems

Many of the strategies discussed in chapters 3 and 5 are still relevant, even in further education, mainly because of the low emotional age of the student with PWS. Nevertheless they may respond well to further, more age-appropriate strategies:

- being given greater personal responsibility and trust as a reward for acceptable behaviour;
- personal counselling;
- group discussions;
- using humour;
- reminding student of previous good behaviour;
- open-door policy for students to discuss grievances with key person;
- writing down feelings and what caused the behaviour.

Residential college is sometimes an option considered by students, teachers and parents, but finding the right option can still be difficult. Intellectually able students may not fit well into residential colleges for those with learning difficulties, yet still find difficulties on an emotional and social level at other types of college, such as those for people with physical disabilities. There are no colleges which specialise specifically in PWS, but there are a few who have had several students, with different levels of success, not just between colleges but also between students – some students have coped better than others.

One of the main areas for concern for those at residential college is weight and dietary control. This can come from two directions:

- the student who comes to college without the experience of a controlled diet at home and is massively obese, and thus needs to lose weight;
- the student who comes to college from a background of strict home and school control and finds their new independence difficult to handle.

Some students are keen to lose weight or maintain their existing weight, and every opportunity should be taken to support and motivate them. Wherever possible, additional exercise sessions should be organised for them at the gym or swimming pool, as well as leisure time options such as walking and dancing. One piece of research contrasted a group of adults with PWS who embarked on an aerobic exercise programme with another group with PWS who did not follow the programme. Those who took part in the exercise showed statistically significant differences in weight loss over a six month period (Silverthorn and Hornak 1993).

For those responsible for the menu planning at college, a booklet has been written specifically for people with PWS which may be helpful (Gellatly 1996).

Other students, however, will try to access food at every opportunity. Coin-operated food machines, waste bins, other students' bedrooms, communal living areas, and even trade delivery vans, are always a source of temptation. Attempts to prevent the student from accessing food will be met with replies such as, 'I can do what I like now I am an adult', or, 'Everyone else has food in their rooms, why can't I?'

These are difficult, if not impossible, questions to answer because ethically and legally the person is within their rights. Cooperation and contracts are a possible answer, working with the student rather against them. In very extreme cases, where the person is posing a severe threat to their own lives or the lives of others there is the possibility of sectioning under the Mental Health Act 1983 (Waters 1996).

Residential colleges

Many residential colleges have the provision for students to move on to semi-independent living in flats, usually shared with other students. This can work well with some students with PWS who are willing to work with their carers towards keeping their weight to a reasonable level. Even then, regular weighing and monitoring is required to ensure that nothing is going amiss. For those whose control around food is minimal, other options may need to be in place, such as closer supervision from staff.

Semi-independent living 'flatlets'

Student study by Tara Chevalier

Vicky is 17 years old and attends a course at a Further Educational Land-based College for post-16 students who have varying degrees of learning/behavioural difficulties. She is now in her second year and has shown considerable progress within this period. She can compose her thoughts and experiences onto paper easily, spelling the majority of words without any help, but she finds it hard to write concisely. Her mathematical ability is also quite good, and last year she achieved a GCSE in Maths (grade D). Unfortunately she is highly competitive and will rush to get the answer first, right or wrong! Her main strength is her determination to improve her learning and carry out tasks, which can also mean that she is very stubborn.

Specific behavioural problems include low tolerance of others, which she is encouraged to control by learning to ignore people she finds hard to deal with, and writing a diary to help release some of these emotions. She gets herself very wound up if things go wrong, so much so that she will end up in tears through sheer frustration. She is encouraged to discuss problems before they get out of control, and to ask for help to keep calm and keep problems in perspective. An area that she finds very hard is understanding other people's views or feelings, as she can only consider her own feelings. Problems regarding food have been minimal, but do include messy, rushed eating, usually in quite large amounts. She is aware of her need to eat healthily and exercise, and is currently participating in an aqua gym programme to help this. Also there has been at least one known occasion where money has been stolen.

To sum up, this student's behaviour has been quite easily managed, especially considering the number of students she has to interact with on a daily basis. On the whole the student has made a lot of progress in controlling her behaviour.

Chapter 8

Further Education: Educational Techniques, Independent Living Skills and Work Placements

At this stage in the educational process, the wide range of intellectual abilities shown by people with PWS becomes very apparent. Some are still unable to read and write, while others will be entering FE with several GCSE passes. Nevertheless, many share the immature emotional and social skills which may be expected in those with severe learning difficulties, but which are also present in those with low average or average abilities, thus posing an obstacle to their progress to employment.

The student with PWS may well find difficulties adapting to the more unstructured format of the further education establishment. They usually work well to a routine, with clear tasks and a full timetable. All the educational techniques which have been suggested for primary and senior levels continue to be appropriate, depending on the ability level of the student. Students are likely to lose concentration fairly quickly in a 'lecturing' situation, often resorting to skin-picking or other obsessional behaviours. Many will do better on project-oriented tasks, practical work, and working on an individual piece of work. Tiredness in the afternoons may still be a problem, as with younger children. Wherever possible, the timetable needs to be geared to reflect this decline, with more taxing lessons scheduled for the morning.

Auditory processing skills and social skills can be helped by asking the person with PWS to interview people in various situations, e.g. for statistics in maths, or for community or media projects.

Table 8.1. shows the strengths and weaknesses of students at FE colleges, as described by lecturers. A comparison with similar tables earlier in this book shows little change from the strengths and weaknesses exhibited by much younger children. However, the weaknesses have tended to become more obvious as the individual gets older, mainly because peers will have 'grown out of' these stages.

One difficulty with some students may be that they are over-confident of their skills, refusing to work at an appropriate level because they see this as boring or beneath their ability. Collaboration with the student is needed here, possibly giving them some work at a higher level so that they can see for themselves where the difficulties lie. On the other hand, some special needs courses are below the level of more able students with PWS, even though they find it difficult to cope with a mainstream course. A mix and match approach may well work here.

The drawings shown in Figures 8.1 and 8.2 (p. 69) were produced by an eighteen year old girl studying art as part of a special needs course at a further education college. Although quite primitive in the mode of

Strengths	Weaknesses
Awareness of own dietary needs/controls own eating	No desire to lose weight and refuses to discuss weight problem
Good relationships with peers	Cannot cope with groups of people
Good relationships with staff	Difficulty with changes to routine
Kind, caring, happy	Unable to recognise dangerous situations
Sense of humour	Low tolerance threshold/temper outbursts
Lively imagination	Unable to see another's point of view
Art	Fantasises events/exaggerates
Good memory	Poor retentive memory for calculations
Maths	Maths
Literacy	Literacy
Writing	Stubborn/uncooperative
Sequencing	Lack of attention/poor concentration
Good general knowledge	Irrelevant/inappropriate responses
Oral communication	Difficulty verbalising emotions when upset by others
Independent living skills	Immature
Well motivated	Disorganised and unpunctual
Perseverance	Easily distressed by minor incidents
Enjoys responsibility	Emotional insecurity and anxiety
Good with young children	Physical activities

Table 8.1 Strengths and weaknesses of further education students, as described by lecturers and teachers in a questionnaire carried out by the PWSA (UK) 1998.

expression, there is great attention to detail. The mouth with its teeth is a motif which occurs many times in her work – perhaps a subconscious expression of her interest in eating. Most of her pictures display a vibrant and imaginative use of colour.

Courses for students with PWS

As all people with PWS are individuals, it is impossible to recommend any particular course for students with PWS. Some of the subjects which people have taken, as reported by parents and teachers, are:

- numeracy and literacy (e.g. Word Power and Number Power);
- cookery;
- safety in the home;
- child care;
- first aid and health care;
- gardening and horticulture;
- IT, word-processing and computing skills;
- life skills;
- woodwork;
- arts and crafts;
- drama;
- environmental studies;

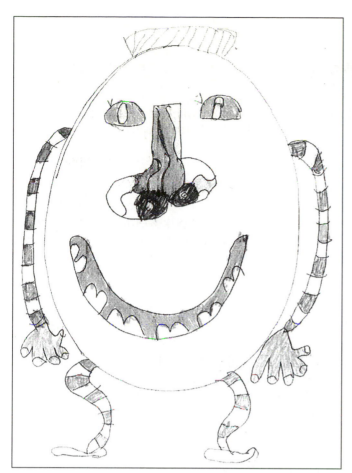

Figure 8.1 The Egg Family. 'I got the idea from an Easter egg pencil case. I drew lots of pictures like this one.'

Figure 8.2 Valentine. 'I drew the big heart first, and then I added in all the little ones to fill up the space.'

- personal care;
- music;
- food hygiene;
- health and safety at work;
- NVQ in Business Admin.

Figure 8.3 shows a student with PWS on a course which includes office skills.

English/literacy

While some students will come to the FE setting with relatively good literacy skills, others may still be barely able to write their own name, and thus the techniques mentioned earlier in the book would be appropriate, including extensive use of computers and word processors. Practical-based projects, research in newspapers and magazines, are likely to prove popular.

Mathematics/ numeracy

Again, the range of ability can be extremely wide by the time FE stage is reached. Some will have a very good grasp of basic number skills, including time and money; others will still require very basic learning concepts, based on practical concrete tasks. One to one teaching may be necessary to keep on task. Techniques used for younger children are still appropriate, especially if these can be coupled with life skills.

Physical education

Although physical education may not form part of the course in a further educational setting, it should be encouraged wherever possible, especially if facilities exist on the campus. Swimming, dance classes, gentle aerobics and weight training are all appropriate, especially if the services of a personal trainer can be engaged.

Figure 8.3 A student with PWS learning office skills.

Independent living skills tend to feature highly in most special needs FE curriculums, but it is important that the course is looked at to see if it needs to be adapted to the needs of the student with PWS.

Independent living skills

Cookery and shopping for food

Always a popular option, this needs to be carefully considered for a student with PWS. Firstly, the decision as to whether this should be an option at all needs to be taken into account and discussed with the student and their parents or carers. Students who have difficulties around food, and cannot be left alone without being tempted to take it, will need special consideration. If they insist on cookery and shopping as an option, it is vital that one to one support is provided to enable them to do this without risk of weight gain or the possibility of stealing items while out shopping.

Some students are able to control themselves when preparing food and are excellent cooks. However, there may need to be home–college liaison to ensure that the products of a cookery session are not consumed before they ever reach home. Food hygiene is also important, as the necessity not to put food into the mouth or handle food can provide a rule which the person with PWS finds easier to understand.

Secondly, the actual content of what is cooked needs consideration. There is sometimes an emphasis on cakes, biscuits, and other high calorie foods, which are inappropriate for a person with PWS. Emphasis should be on healthy eating, with menus which include salad preparation, pasta dishes and low fat meals. If there are several students with weight problems, it may be possible to devise a special course for those wanting to lose weight – there is no need to single out the person with PWS: many students with special needs have problems with their weight.

Other considerations around food are discussed in Chapter 7.

Handling money

This is another potential minefield for students with PWS. Many are able to learn how to write cheques and are capable of opening a bank account, and most, apart from the least intellectually able, are also legally entitled to collect their own benefits and allowances.

However, they are vulnerable to other students bullying them into handing money over, as well as to the temptation to spend the money on extra food items. One way round this is to ensure that receipts are obtained for all purchases, and checked off against cash in the purse or in the account. Keeping receipts also helps with budgeting.

Work placements or work experience should be given careful consideration, and potential employers should be warned of any tendencies on the part of some students to steal food or money. People with PWS are generally very keen to please, and eager to become useful members of society, but they can sometimes let themselves down by

Work placements and training options

giving way to the temptation to steal food or money. They should not be set up to fail. For instance, it would be unfair to place someone who could not control their food intake in a cafe or canteen situation – even if it were only clearing tables and washing dishes: the opportunity to sneak food from leftovers and the garbage will undoubtedly be taken. Equally, potential employers should be warned not to leave food or money around. It does not take much to ensure that such items are locked away out of sight.

Other, less obvious, temptations can occur in other work experience situations. A placement in a playgroup may seem ideal, but not if the children's biscuits and milk are proving too tempting to the person with PWS. While someone who wants to work in this environment should not be discouraged, it is important that issues around food are addressed before the person takes up their placement, both with the employer and the person themselves.

The range of potential work placements and training is very wide. Parents have reported the following:

- car washing;
- helping in a nursing home;
- shelf stacking;
- working in an animal rescue centre;
- catering;
- shop work, especially charity shops;
- helping in playgroups or creches;
- conservation work;
- office work – filing, photocopying, collating leaflets.

Work

Sometimes people with PWS leave college with high expectations, particularly if they have been successful in obtaining certificates and qualifications. Unfortunately, employers tend to have less patience with their lack of social skills, emotional immaturity, and tiredness at the end of the day. It can come as a big shock to the person that they cannot find a job in the area they would like to work in, and students may need counselling around this issue before they leave college.

However, some instances of people doing paid work have been reported. These include packing, craft work and office work. Parents have also reported a range of voluntary tasks being undertaken, similar to those given in the list of work experience above. Many, however, go on to Adult Training Centres or Social Education Centres, or remain at home (Waters *et al.* 1990).

Whilst most people with PWS are unable to find paid employment once they leave college, many do voluntary work or attend social activity centres.

Barry is 18 years old and attends a course at the same college as Vicky in the previous chapter. He is now in his second year. Despite having very obvious physical traits associated with PWS, he shows very few of the behavioural traits. He finds it very hard to discuss emotional issues, which as a result turn into problems that he cannot cope with on his own. At such time he has great difficulty in controlling his emotional state and is unable to explain what the problem is without crying uncontrollably. Regarding strengths in his character, he is a very determined young man without being stubborn. Eating behaviour has not been a problem, although given the opportunity he would spend any money on food that he is obviously not allowed at home, e.g. chips, chocolate, and eat his lunch, although there has not been a case of theft.

His reading abilities are very poor. He can read basic common words only, although he has managed to remember a selection of words learned in sessions from week to week. He is encouraged to read more and to ask for clarification if unsure of a word. He also enjoys trying to remember spellings from week to week, which again has meant that he builds his vocabulary very slowly. He is particularly good at sums involving adding and subtraction, and enjoys doing these, although the answers are achieved by using his fingers. He is currently being encouraged to count on so that he can do sums quickly, and to add/subtract numbers in multiples, which will in turn lead him to become better at handling money. He is very keen to do other mathematical sums but requires a lot of support, and will unfortunately forget methods from week to week in most cases. The most difficult area for him is to judge his performance and his needs, as he thinks everything is easy.

On the whole, this student is a pleasure to teach and tries hard in most things he does.

Student study by Tara Chevalier

Chapter 9

The Future For Youngsters with Prader-Willi Syndrome

Considerable steps forward have been taken in the past 20 years to ensure that the needs of people with PWS are recognised by the statutory authorities and the community at large, but there is still much more to be done. There has been increasing interest in PWS-specific group homes for those who wish to leave the parental home, and a few are now in operation. Nevertheless, there should still be choices for those who do not wish to live with others with PWS, and these will need extra support.

All too often, young people leave school or college with unrealistic expectations about what the world has to offer them, and can become very depressed when their hopes are dashed. While it would be naive to think that these young people could ever get to the top of a career ladder, there are still plenty of interesting and useful opportunities they could access, if only society was more prepared to make allowances. On the other hand, the more able a young person is to function within society as it exists, the more likely they are to succeed, and education plays a large part in providing this ability.

Children and young people with PWS need a very special environment in which to flourish, and if this is in place, they can go on to live long, healthy and productive lives. It is hoped that, with better knowledge and management, a generation of children is now growing up who will not have follow in the footsteps of the young woman who left school 10 years ago at the age of 16, and whose mother wrote:

My daughter was never asked to stay on from her school days. People never had the time to put themselves out to help her. She did voluntary work, working with children for £6 a week (that included her bus fare). And then when she was getting worse with her PWS and diabetes they got rid of her and she has never done anything since. She felt so rejected. I hope with all my heart that so many things can change for the future of PWS people because they need all the help they can get and so do the parents.

The indications are that nowadays people are more willing to try to understand PWS, and to pass that understanding to the youngsters in their care. One young woman currently at residential college has spent her whole life in schools where a supportive environment was in place, and her dietary needs were well supervised. She is now able to advise her enablers at college about her needs in an informed and usually reasonable manner. The fine-tuning of her needs is taking time, but all are committed to providing the best possible support for her, and her future is looking very positive.

Teachers have a very important role to play in the lives of people with PWS, whatever stage of their education they are at. With good understanding and support during their time in education, youngsters with PWS are better equipped to take their place in the world outside, to reach their full potential, and to be able to look forward to a long and healthy life.

Useful Addresses

Prader-Willi Syndrome Association (UK)
33 Leopold St
Derby
DE1 2HF
Website: www.pwsa-uk.demon.co.uk

Prader-Willi Syndrome Association (USA)
5700 Midnight Pass Road, Suite 6
Sarasota
Florida 34242
United States of America
Website: www.pwsausa.org

Prader-Willi Syndrome Association of Australia
(for information on State Associations)
8 North Tce
Ardrossan
South Australia 5571
Australia

Prader-Willi Syndrome Association (New Zealand) Inc
PO Box 143
Masterton
New Zealand
email:pwsanz@xtra.co.uz

Prader-Willi Syndrome Association, Canada
c/o McMaster University Medical Centre
Rm 2V12, 1200 Main Street West
Hamilton
Ontario L8N 3Z5
Canada

International Prader-Willi Syndrome Organisation
Website: www.ipwso.suite.dk
(lists all international PWS associations, and has
up-to-date scientific information)

References

Akefeldt, A., Akefeldt, B., Gillberg, C. (1997) 'Voice, speech and language characteristics of children with Prader-Willi syndrome', *Journal of Intellectual Disability Research* **41** (4), 302–11.

Bhargava, S. A. *et al.* (1996) 'Rectal bleeding in Prader-Willi sydnrome', *Pediatrics* **97** (2), 265–7.

Borghgraef, M., Fryns, J.-P., Van den Berghe, H. (1990) 'Psychological profile and behavioural characteristics in 12 patients with Prader-Willi syndrome', *Genetic Counseling* **38** (2), 141–50.

Carpenter, P. K. (1994) 'Prader-Willi syndrome in old age', *Journal of Intellectual Disability Reseach* **38**, 529–31.

Cassidy, S. B. *et al.* (1995) 'Few phenotypic differences between patients with Prader-Willi syndrome due to deletion 15q and uniparental disomy 15 (summary)', *The Gathered View* **XX** (6), 5.

Clarke, D. J., Webb, T., Bachmann-Clarke, J.P. (1995) 'Prader-Willi syndrome and psychotic symptoms: report of a further case', *Irish Journal of Psychological Medicine* **12** (1), 27–9.

Crnic, K. A. *et al.* (1980) 'Preventing mental retardation associated with gross obesity in the Prader-Willi syndrome', *Pediatrics* **66**, 787–9.

Curfs, L. M. G. *et al.* (1991) 'Strengths and weaknesses in the cognitive profile of youngsters with Prader-Willi Syndrome', *Clinical Genetics* **40** (6), 430–4.

Curfs, L. M. G. *et al.* (1995) 'Personality profiles of youngsters with Prader-Willi syndrome and youngsters attending regular schools', *Journal of Intellectual Disability Research* **39** (3), 241–48.

Downey, D. A. and Knutson, C. L. (1995) 'Speech and language issues' in Greenswag, L. R. and Alexander, R. C. (eds) *Management of Prader-Willi Syndrome (Second Edition)*, 142–155. New York: Springer-Verlag.

Dykens, E. M. *et al.* (1992) 'Profiles, correlates, and trajectories of intelligence in Prader-Willi syndrome', *Journal of the American Academy of Child and Adolescent Psychiatry* **31** (6), 1125–30.

Dykens, E. M. and Cassidy, S. B. (1995) 'Correlates of maladaptive behavior in children and adults with Prader-Willi syndrome', *American Journal of Medical Genetics (Neuropsychiatric Genetics)* **60**, 546–9.

Dykens, E. M. and Kasari, C. (1997) 'Maladaptive behavior in children with Prader-Willi Syndrome, Down Syndrome, and nonspecific mental retardation', *American Journal on Mental Retardation* **102** (3), 228–37.

Dykens, E. M., Leckman, J., Cassidy, S. B. (1996) 'Obsessions and compulsions in Prader-Willi Syndrome', *Journal of Child Psychology and Psychiatry* **37** (8), 995–1002.

Eiholzer, U. *et al.* (1998) 'Treatment with human growth hormone in patients with Prader-Labhart-Willi syndrome reduces body fat and increases muscle mass and physical performance', *European Journal of Paediatrics* **157** 368–77.

Gabel, S. *et al.* (1986) 'Neuropsychological capacity of Prader-Willi children: general and specific aspects of impairment', *Applied Research in Mental Retardation* **7**, 459–66.

Gellatly, M. S. N. (1996) *Prader-Willi Syndrome: Food and Health.* Prader-Willi Syndrome Association (UK).

Goodger, D., Langlands, L., Almond, L (1996) 'Educating the child with Prader-Willi Syndrome' in Williams, A. and Waters, J. (eds) *Prader-Willi Syndrome – The Best of Training Days*, 57–66. PWSA (UK).

Hanchett, J. M. *et al.* (1992) 'A comparison of characteristics in 33 Japanese and 83 American patients with Prader-Willi syndrome', in Cassidy, S.B. (ed.) *Prader-Willi syndrome and other chromosome 15q deletion disorders*, 147–151. New York: Springer-Verlag.

Holland, A. J. (1998) 'Understanding the eating disorder affecting people with Prader-Willi syndrome', *Journal of Applied Research in Intellectual Disabilities* **11** (3), 192–206.

Holm, V. A. *et al.* (1993) 'Prader-Willi syndrome; consensus diagnostic criteria', *Pediatrics* **91**, 398-402.

James, T. N. (1985) 'The Prader-Willi syndrome adolescent in an educational setting', *Journal of Practical Approaches to Developmental Handicap* **9** (2), 13–17.

James, T. N. and Brown, R. I. (1992) *Prader-Willi Syndrome – Home, School and Community.* London: Chapman and Hall.

Kleppe, S. A. *et al.* (1990) 'The speech and language characteristics of children with Prader-Willi syndrome', *Journal of Speech and Hearing Disorders* **55**, 300–9.

Laurance, B.M. (1961) 'Hypotonia, hypogonadism and mental retardation in childhood', *Archives of Disease in Childhood* **36**, 690.

Lloyd, E. T. and Deusterhaus-Minor, M. A. (1995) 'Physical and Occupational Therapy' in Greenswag, L. R. and Alexander, R. C. (eds) *Management of Prader-Willi Syndrome (Second Edition)*, 115–22. New York: Springer-Verlag.

Prader, A., Labhart, A., Willi, H. (1956) 'Ein syndrom von adipositas, kleinwuchs, kryptorchismus und oligophrenie nach myotonier-artigem zustand in neugeborenalter', *Schweizerische Medizinische Wochenschrift* **86**, 1260–1.

Silverthorn, K. H. and Hornak, J. E. (1993) 'Beneficial effects of exercise on aerobic capacity and body composition in adults with Prader-Willi syndrome', *American Journal on Mental Retardation* **97** (6), 654–8.

Taylor, R. L. (1988) 'Cognitive and Behavioral Characteristics' in Caldwell, M. L. and Taylor, R. L. (eds) *Prader-Willi Syndrome – Selected Research and Management Issues*, 29–42. New York: Springer-Verlag.

van Lieshout, C. F. M. *et al.* (1998) 'Problem behaviors and personality of children and adolescents with Prader-Willi syndrome', *Journal of Pediatric Psychology* **23** (2), 111–20.

Vela-Bueno, A. (1984) 'Sleep in the Prader-Willi Syndrome – clinical and polygraphic findings', *Arch. Neurol.* **41**, 294–6.

Ward, O. C. (1997) 'Down's 1864 case of Prader-Willi syndrome: a follow-up report', *Journal of the Royal Society of Medicine* **90**, 694–4.

Watanabe, H., Ohmori, O., Abe, K. (1997) 'Recurrent brief depression in Prader-Willi syndrome: a case report', *Psychiatric Genetics* **7**, 41–4.

Waters, J. (ed.) (1991) *Report on a Study Day on Educating Children and Teenagers with Prader-Willi Syndrome.* Prader-Willi Syndrome Association (UK).

Waters, J. (ed.) (1993) 'Appendix 3(a)', *Report on two Multidisciplinary Training Days on Prader-Willi Syndrome held at Ninewells Hospital, Dundee.* Prader-Willi Syndrome Association (UK).

Waters, J. (1996) *A Handbook for Parents and Carers of Adults with Prader-Willi Syndrome (Revised Edition).* Prader-Willi Syndrome Association (UK).

Waters, J. (ed.) (1999) *Our Way of Life – An Information Pack Produced in Cooperation with People with PWS for People with PWS.* Prader-Willi Syndrome Association (UK).

Waters, J., Clarke, D. J., Corbett, J. A. (1990) 'Educational and occupational outcome in Prader-Willi syndrome', *Child: Care, Health and Development* **16**, 271–82.

Whitman, B. (1993) 'Ask the professional – repetitive verbalizations', *The Gathered View* **XVIII** (1), 9–10.

Whitman, B. and Greenswag, L. R. (1995) 'Psychological and Behavioral Management' in Greenswag, L. R. and Alexander, R. C. (eds) *Management of Prader-Willi Syndrome (Second Edition)*, 125–41. New York: Springer-Verlag.

Whyte, F. (1998) 'Prader-Willi syndrome', *Royal College of Speech and Language Therapists Bulletin*, October, 9–10.

Williams, T. (1996) 'Statementing and social skills training for a child with PWS', *Prader-Willi Syndrome Association (UK) News* **48**, 14–16.

Note: *The Gathered View* is the official newsletter of the Prader-Willi Syndrome Association (USA).

Prader-Willi Syndrome Association (UK) News is the official magazine of the Prader-Willi Syndrome Association (UK)

Index